The Pocket Anabaptist

The Pocket Anabaptist

A Concise Systematic Theology
of the Radical Reformation

CODY COOK

WIPF & STOCK · Eugene, Oregon

THE POCKET ANABAPTIST
A Concise Systematic Theology of the Radical Reformation

Wipf & Stock
An Imprint of Wipf and Stock Publishers
199 W. 8th Ave., Suite 3
Eugene, OR 97401

www.wipfandstock.com

PAPERBACK ISBN: 979-8-3852-4270-2
HARDCOVER ISBN: 979-8-3852-4271-9
EBOOK ISBN: 979-8-3852-4272-6

VERSION NUMBER 013025

Contents

Abbreviations

13A—The Thirteen Articles (1626). Sought to provide a mediating statement between "outer word" Christians who emphasized sola scriptura and "inner word" Christians who valued the illumination of the Holy Spirit in the lives of believers. The translation quoted in this volume is from Koop, Karl, ed. *Confessions of Faith in the Anabaptist Tradition: 1527–1676*.

33A—The Thirty-Three Articles (1617). One of the most extensive early Anabaptist confessions. Represents the views of conservative Dutch Mennonites. The translation quoted in this volume is from Koop, Karl, ed. *Confessions of Faith in the Anabaptist Tradition: 1527–1676*.

AIO—*Anabaptism in Outline* (2019). A collection of quotations from early Anabaptist leaders arranged topically. I have used the editor's numbering system so that you can easily find any quotation I use regardless of whether you are using a physical or digital edition. Klaassen, Walter, ed. *Anabaptism in Outline*.

BJL—The Blasphemy of John of Leiden (1535). The translation quoted in this volume is from Wenger, J. C. *The Complete Writings of Menno Simons: c.1496–1561*.

CC—Concept of Cologne (1591). Sought to find a middle way between opposing factions on how strictly to enforce the ban in matters of church discipline. The translation quoted in this volume is from Koop, Karl, ed. *Confessions of Faith in the Anabaptist Tradition: 1527–1676*.

CDS—Confession of the Distressed Christians (1552). The translation quoted in this volume is from Wenger, J. C. *The Complete Writings of Menno Simons*: c.1496–1561.

CH—Swiss Brethren Confession of Hesse (1578). Drafted by Anabaptists in the German territory of Hesse. Though a statement of Anabaptists beliefs, it was also intended to present a positive face of the movement to Lutheran authorities. For this reason, it includes positive statements about the role of government authorities but leaves out references to nonviolence and the Anabaptist rejection of the sword–themes which were common in other Anabaptist confessions. The translation quoted in this volume is from Koop, Karl, ed. *Confessions of Faith in the Anabaptist Tradition: 1527–1676*.

CJC—The Confession of Jan Cents (1630). Meant to bring together United Frisian, Flemish, and High German Anabaptists, this statement reflected the views of various Anabaptists but was likely written primarily by Jan Cents. It holds to a strong view of church discipline and the Melchiorite doctrine of the incarnation, that Jesus' flesh did not come from Mary but was heavenly in origin. The translation quoted in this volume is from Koop, Karl, ed. *Confessions of Faith in the Anabaptist Tradition: 1527–1676*.

CO—Congregational Order (1527?). Gave guidance for how Anabaptist Christians were to live together. Though no authorship is given, it is Swiss in origin. The translation quoted in this volume is from Koop, Karl, ed. *Confessions of Faith in the Anabaptist Tradition: 1527–1676*.

DC—Dordrecht Confession (1632). Meant to bring together United Frisian, Flemish, and High German Anabaptists, though most of its signers were Flemish. The translation quoted in this volume is from Koop, Karl, ed. *Confessions of Faith in the Anabaptist Tradition: 1527–1676*.

HCF—(1542). Riedemann, Peter. *Peter Riedemann's Hutterite Confession of Faith*. Translated by John Friesen.

KC—Kempen Confession (1545). Drafted by Anabaptists under the influence of Menno Simons and presented to more tolerant authorities at Kempen. The translation quoted in this volume is from Koop, Karl, ed. *Confessions of Faith in the Anabaptist Tradition: 1527–1676.*

LLF—Love Is Like Fire (1993). An organized translation of the Hutterite theologian Peter Riedemann's early prison works. Riedemann, Peter. *Love Is like Fire: The Confession of an Anabaptist Prisoner.* Emmy Barth Maendel, ed.

LMS—A collection of writings from the early Anabaptist leader Michael Sattler. Sattler, Michael. *The Legacy of Michael Sattler.* John Howard Yoder, ed.

PC—Prussian Confession (1660). Written by Prussian Mennonites, possibly to present their views to German authorities. The translation quoted in this volume is from Koop, Karl, ed. *Confessions of Faith in the Anabaptist Tradition: 1527–1676.*

PM—*The Writings of Pilgram Marpeck* (2019). William Klassen and Walter Klaassen, trans.

SA—Schleithem Articles/Brotherly Union (1527). Perhaps the most well known Anabaptist confession. Michael Sattler considered its primary author. He was arrested shortly after the conference and executed. The translation quoted in this volume is from Koop, Karl, ed. *Confessions of Faith in the Anabaptist Tradition: 1527–1676.*

SC—Short Confession of Faith and the Essential Elements of Christian Doctrine (1610). Sought to unify Waterlander Anabaptists and English Separatists. More mystical in nature than most Anabaptist confessions. The translation quoted in this volume is from Koop, Karl, ed. *Confessions of Faith in the Anabaptist Tradition: 1527–1676.*

TCF—The True Christian Faith (1541). The translation quoted in this volume is from Wenger, J. C. *The Complete Writings of Menno Simons: c.1496–1561.*

WA—Wismar Articles (1554). Drafted by Anabaptist leaders looking for common ground on issues related to church discipline. The translation quoted in this volume is from Koop, Karl, ed. *Confessions of Faith in the Anabaptist Tradition: 1527-1676.*

WC—Waterlander Confession (1577). A fairly thorough doctrinal statement from Holland Anabaptists which challenged the Calvinist beliefs which were spreading to the region and held to a more moderate form of church discipline. The translation quoted in this volume is from Koop, Karl, ed. *Confessions of Faith in the Anabaptist Tradition: 1527-1676.*

Introduction

In Rottenburg, Germany, in the year 1527, a former monk turned religious radical was on trial for heresy. His name was Michael Sattler. As the charges were read against him, he responded with clarity of conviction. He was accused of opposing infant baptism, the Roman Catholic doctrine of transubstantiation, imperial mandates, and making unpatriotic statements. He answered eloquently, explaining his Anabaptist views and detailing their foundation in Scripture. His judges responded that they were not willing to debate with him, but the hangman would.

Sattler knew what he believed and was able to defend it to others. This sure knowledge of his doctrine gave him the conviction to die for it. His words before those who condemned him to death helped to shape the convictions of the radical wing of the Reformation—the Anabaptists.

Though largely known today by its small, peculiar, separatist groups like the technology-rejecting Amish, the plain clothes-wearing Mennonites, and the private property-eschewing Hutterites, Anabaptist Christianity has attracted a surge of interest in recent decades. Their emphasis on simplicity, nonviolence, and community has been particularly attractive to evangelicals fatigued by war fever, crass commercialism, and the isolation and loneliness which often flows from our cultural individualism. As more and more Christians from mainstream evangelical backgrounds have begun to identify with Anabaptism, some (like Stuart Murray in his book *The Naked Anabaptist*) have sought to explain what it

1

is at its core and why it has appealed to so many different types of Christians.

Anabaptism emerged from the western Christian tradition, sharing values with Catholic and Protestant Christians but also diverging on significant issues. The mainstream Anabaptist movement agreed with Catholics and Protestants on the central points presented in the Apostles' and Nicene creeds, but their distinctives have tended to center around the importance of a voluntary, sincere, and obedient faith lived out in Christian community. In 1943, Harold S. Bender summarized the "Anabaptist vision" with three points:

> First, a new conception of the essence of Christianity as discipleship; second, a new conception of the church as a brotherhood; and third, a new ethic of love and nonresistance.[1]

One key idea that held Anabaptists together was their belief in adult baptism (from which the movement's name was derived—*Ana-baptist* or re-baptizer). Another shared value was nonviolence. Not all of the earliest Anabaptists were nonresistant (a term for Anabaptist pacifism rooted in Christ's command to not resist an evil person in Matt 5:39), but over time a consensus was reached on the rejection of violence and the importance of voluntary religion. Early Anabaptist leader Pilgram Marpeck described Anabaptist congregations in this way:

> There is no coercion, but rather a voluntary spirit in Christ Jesus our Lord. Whoever does not desire [this spirit] let him remain outside; whoever desires it let him come and drink freely, without price (PM, III).

Early Anabaptism began as three distinct but cross-pollinating movements—Swiss, Southern German-Austrian, and Dutch.

The Swiss movement began under the influence of, and later outright rejection by, the Protestant reformer Ulrich Zwingli. Zwingli was a rabble-rouser in the city of Zurich, challenging mandated tithes and infant baptism at first, then moderating

---

1. Bender, *Anabaptist Vision*.

his positions once he was given a voice in local government. As some of his followers and associates (like Conrad Grebel and Felix Mantz) grew tired of his compromises, they decided to take a stand—they refused to baptize their infants and re-baptized each other as adults. From there they went out preaching this doctrine of a sincere, believing church, rejecting the nominal civil church which they believed infant baptism brought about. At this early stage, some of the Swiss Anabaptists, like Grebel, embraced pacifism—though not all.

In 1527, Mantz was sentenced to death by drowning by the Zurich city council. That same year, the German Anabaptist Michael Sattler chaired a meeting of the Swiss Brethren that produced the Schleitheim Confession—an early Anabaptist statement of beliefs and practices that promoted nonviolence and separation from the state.

Early important figures among the South German-Austrian Anabaptists include Hans Denck and Hans Hut. Hut was particularly focused on eschatology, believing his generation to be in the last days. He taught pacifism as an interim ethic, believing that at the very end (which was coming soon) the true Christians would slay the godless with the sword. Denck was trained in the biblical languages but veered toward more spiritualist forms of religion as opposed to more biblically-rooted approaches. By the time he died (of the plague), he had abandoned the requirement of water baptism—thus moving out of Anabaptism entirely.

There were also South German-Austrian Anabaptists who were more orthodox and less apocalyptically obsessed, though they differed on other points of doctrine. Hutterite leaders like Jakob Hutter and Peter Riedemann were fairly radical—teaching pacifism and the practice of shared goods within Christian communities. The more conventional Balthasar Hubmaier allowed for Christian participation in state violence, assuming the cause was defensive and just. Seeking a more balanced moderate approach, Pilgram Marpeck rejected state violence but still served the state in nonviolent civic functions.

In the Netherlands, Menno Simons and Dirk Philips emerged as major figures—both embracing pacifism as well as the heterodox doctrine of Christ's "heavenly flesh," which was taught by Melchior Hoffman (more on that when we get to Christology). Other Anabaptist leaders from the Netherlands included Jan Matthijs and Jan van Leyden, who took the city of Münster by force and proclaimed that the end had come. Under the influence of these Münsterite Anabaptists, money was abolished, polygamy was promoted, and everyone was required to leave their doors open at all times to promote brotherhood and the sharing of all things. Eventually the city was retaken at a great loss of life. Over time, Netherlands Anabaptism coalesced around the Mennonite doctrine of pacifism and the "heavenly flesh" doctrine fell away as Mennonite beliefs became more orthodox.

Finally, as early Anabaptism spread to Poland and Italy, it tended to take on more unitarian and humanistic forms, opposing orthodox Christian beliefs.

How Are We Defining an Anabaptist?

In light of the diversity of groups that have historically identified as or associated with Anabaptists, an overly inclusive definition of Anabaptism would be particularly difficult to summarize in a work such as this. For that reason, I will be narrowing my focus to those early groups and figures whose beliefs and practices have defined core Anabaptist values over time *and* which fit into the broader orthodox Christian tradition as defined by the Nicene Creed. To be more specific, my criteria for defining an Anabaptist group or leader in this book, unless otherwise noted or qualified, is as follows:

1. They hold to believers' baptism.

2. They reject violence and are at least suspicious of Christian participation in the state.

3. They are confessionally Christian. In particular, they are Trinitarian and affirm the unique, divine inspiration of Scripture.

These criteria would exclude the violent Münsterite Anabaptists as well as unitarian and spiritualist Anabaptists such as Hans Denck and early Polish and Italian groups. However, there are some borderline figures that I have included in this volume. For instance, Menno Simons and Dirk Philips held to the heterodox "heavenly flesh" view of Jesus. However, due to their broader orthodoxy and ongoing influence upon the Anabaptist movement, they cannot be excluded from a treatment like this one. Also included are occasional citations from the influential Anabaptist theologian Balthasar Hubmaier. Hubmaier affirmed the limited use of the sword by Christians on behalf of the state, though as an Anabaptist he believed in the importance of Christian conscience which caused him to affirm a greater separation of church and state than Lutherans and Reformed Christians.

Are Anabaptists Protestants?

Western Christianity is often divided into two categories—Catholic and Protestant. Historian C. Arnold Snyder noted that Anabaptists held "spiritual ideals common in monasticism and late medieval piety,"[2] so Catholicism is certainly in Anabaptist blood. However, because Anabaptists shared many of Luther's objections to the Roman Catholic Church and were influenced by his movement, they are often considered to be just another branch of the Protestant tree.

While a case can be made for Anabaptism as part of the Protestant movement, perhaps a stronger case can be made for Anabaptists as a third category distinct from but influenced by both Catholicism and Protestantism. Anabaptists were not part of the so-called Magisterial Reformation of Luther, Calvin, and Zwingli but were a major stream in the *Radical Reformation*.

---

2. Koop, *Confessions of Faith in the Anabaptist Tradition*, loc. 375. It is of note that some early Anabaptist leaders came to the movement from Catholicism—Sattler, Schiemer, and Simons had been priests. However, others (like Hubmaier and Grebel) came to Anabaptism through Magisterial Reformation movements.

One major belief that made the Anabaptists seem particularly radical was their rejection of the state church model—a model which both Catholics and Protestants were eager to embrace and put to work for their respective parties. In fact, the word "protestant" derived from a letter of protestation signed by German princes defending the Lutheran doctrine. William McGrath summarized their protestation this way—that they

> wanted to manage the religious affairs of their own territories as they saw fit, without any interference from Rome, or any other "higher power,"—when an emperor denied them this right, they protested, and insisted on making the Church in their territories a department of the government, as the post office is in America.[3]

While many Protestant churches today practice believers' baptism only, the Anabaptist insistence upon believers' baptism strongly distinguished them from the infant-baptizing Protestants of the 16th century. Because infant baptism served to join a newborn human to the Christian nation into which they were born, Anabaptists understood their position on baptism as a natural outworking of their belief in voluntary Christianity.

The Anabaptists also took issue with the Protestant formulation of "faith alone," which they perceived as providing cover for sin. Peter Riedemann laid this charge against the Magisterial Reformation:

> Many people, especially Lutherans, say that Christ is their righteousness and goodness even though they still lead abominable and impure lives. To speak like this is to give lip service to God, but to be far removed from him in their hearts. It leads people away from Christ rather than toward him, because in this manner people are prevented from striving for true righteousness, which is only in Christ. They continue in their sins for ever and ever (HCF).

---

3. McGrath, "Anabaptists: Neither Catholic nor Protestant," para. 1.

Nevertheless, many modern Anabaptists have taken a more brotherly attitude toward Protestants and even embraced the term "evangelical" for themselves. This shift toward Protestantism has likely only been possible because many Protestants have also shifted toward Anabaptist convictions regarding freedom of religion and the necessity of holy living.

Thus, whether or not Anabaptists should be considered part of Protestantism may be a matter of perspective. As we uncover the early movement's major beliefs and practices, we will discover a faith which can be both compared to and contrasted with the major western Christianities of Protestantism and Roman Catholicism.

Why a systematic theology?

The enterprise of systematic theology has fallen on some hard times. Those defending it must fight a war on at least three fronts:

1. Against theological liberals who deny that scripture speaks in a united voice on any topic, so no systematic effort can be made to summarize it.

2. Against biblical theologians who prefer to trace the development of major themes throughout Scripture rather than treat it as a flat document which we can extract propositions from at will.

3. Against the anti-fundamentalists who fear that systematic theology creates a feedback loop wherein we read our preconceived dogmatic conclusions *into* Scripture rather than exegeting them *from* Scripture.

While I am not sympathetic to the objections raised by the first group, I think the concerns of the second and third are quite legitimate. However, systematic theology can still be useful if we keep their concerns in mind. Here is the methodology for how I will approach this effort:

1. This book will be a descriptive and *historical* systematic theology which will collect common answers from Anabaptist confessions and leaders when it comes to questions relevant to systematic and dogmatic theology. While I am not opposed to systematic theologies of the Bible, this will actually be a systematic theology of 16th-century orthodox Anabaptist Christianity.

2. I will also highlight areas where the answers given by these early Anabaptists could benefit from further development in dialogue with the insights of other Christian traditions and modern scholarship.

Just because I present an Anabaptist answer to a question relevant to systematics does not mean that I think it is necessarily the *best* answer. While I fit broadly within the orthodox Anabaptist tradition, I am a Christian first and feel no obligation to side with Anabaptist answers over other traditions when I assess the former to be insufficiently biblical or overly dogmatic. This is consistent with the Anabaptist spirit of questioning received traditions to see if they line up with Scripture and good sense. I concur with Koop's assessment, which encourages us to remember that retrieving the apostolic faith and applying it to our current context is an ongoing process:

> Anabaptists [*sic*] communities were never able to jump back 1,500 years of history and reject the mediation of tradition, nor were they able to develop their theology in isolation from the surrounding religious milieu, which was both Catholic and Protestant in character. And, of course, no confessional statements were produced by Anabaptist groups without the influence of wider historical, social and cultural factors.[4]

Some readers may be asking whether an Anabaptist systematic theology can even be written. It has become popular since Bender's essay *The Anabaptist Vision* to see Anabaptist Christianity as "a life patterned after the teaching and example of Christ" as

---

4. Koop, *Confessions of Faith in the Anabaptist Tradition*, loc. 387.

opposed to taking a systematic approach which makes religion "a matter of intellect, of doctrinal belief."[5] However, this is not only a shallow reading of Bender but also of Anabaptism.

While Reformed Christianity has certainly given the world far more in the vein of systematic theologies, early Anabaptism produced numerous systematic confessions. Dirk Philips's *Enchiridion* and Peter Riedemann's *Confession of Faith* stand out as particularly lengthy early Anabaptist treatments of theology that are fairly systematic. Of early Anabaptist confessions, Koop writes that they "have been an integral dimension of Anabaptist expression . . . It is possible that adherents of Anabaptism produced more confessions of faith than any other Protestant stream."[6]

In addition to the confessions developed by early Anabaptist communities, the Apostles' and Nicene Creeds took on a significant role in defining Christianity for them. For instance, Balthasar Hubmaier's baptismal order required a confession of belief in the ancient creed *prior* to the candidate pledging to renounce the devil and his works, thus placing belief in orthodoxy as a precondition for a pledge to commit to discipleship. Then, finally, the candidate could be baptized and officially incorporated into the church.

Since confessions played such a significant role in the early Anabaptist movement, it is surprising how little attention they have received in contemporary Anabaptist scholarship. Why is this the case? Koop muses:

> It has sometimes been assumed that Anabaptists were non-creedal and non-confessional, that they emphasized ethics rather than doctrine, that their theology was implicit rather than explicit. Given these assumptions, it is not surprising that scholars have often failed to recognize the significance of the confessional tradition.[7]

While this assumption that Anabaptists were non-creedal cannot be fully supported by the historical data, those who see

5. Bender, *Anabaptist Vision*.
6. Koop, *Confessions of Faith in the Anabaptist Tradition*, loc. 134.
7. Koop, *Confessions of Faith in the Anabaptist Tradition*, loc. 161.

Anabaptism as ethical rather than doctrinal are overstating something that truly is in early Anabaptism—that these radical Christians were very practical about their doctrine. In this tradition there is not a nice, clean line between theory and practice (or faith and works), as Protestant theology often seems to suggest there should be. Therefore, an Anabaptist attempt at systematic theology will likely incorporate ethics and practical theology much more than traditional Protestant efforts, as this one does.

1. Scripture

EARLY ANABAPTISTS OFTEN MADE a distinction between the "outer word" of Scripture and the "inner word" of God's voice to our souls. Some Anabaptists, like Hans Denck, emphasized the inner word so much that Scripture became significantly diminished in prominence.

However, for the orthodox Anabaptists whose theology has lived on in mainstream Anabaptism, all of Scripture was seen as divinely inspired and authoritative, though a particular emphasis was placed on those Scriptures that provided more direct guidance for living in the new covenant era.

Our Authority

Early Anabaptist confessions acknowledge that "the holy Scriptures, both Old and New Testaments, were ordered by God to be written, and that they were written by holy men driven by the Spirit of God" (CH). As a result, Christians "should therefore use the Scriptures for teaching, admonition, for discipline and improvement, and to demonstrate that the foundation of their faith is in harmony with the Scriptures" (CH). Instead of the swords which Protestant and Roman Catholic authorities often used to defend their position, Anabaptists believed that "the weapon of the faithful . . . is alone the powerful, holy, saving word of God" (KC).

Menno Simons concurred. He wrote that the Scriptures "are the true scepter and rule by which the Lord's kingdom, house, church, and congregation must be ruled and governed." Since Scripture was the standard, all doctrines and practices contrary to it "should be measured by this infallible rule and demolished by this just and divine scepter, and destroyed without any respect of persons" (AIO 7.9).

Since Anabaptists were particularly focused on living out their Christian faith in community, the biblical passages which spoke to this concern were given special prominence. Thus, while commands regarding temple sacrifices and ancient Israel's war-making were seen as inspired, they were not quite as relevant as Christ's Sermon On The Mount. As a result, while all Scripture is inspired, in actual practice parts of it took on more significance. Leonhard Schiemer stated this principle in a dramatic way that would floor a modern evangelical, and probably many of his Anabaptist contemporaries:

> When you read, read mostly in the New Testament and the Psalms. You must know that God spoke to the Jews through Moses and the prophets in a hidden manner. But when Christ himself came, he and his apostles illuminated all things with a much clearer understanding... Although it is good to read in the prophets and in the books of the kings and Moses it is not really necessary. One finds everything in the New Testament (AIO 7.4).

Riedeman took a more moderate approach—downgrading the old *covenant* as inferior but not the Old *Testament*, which God revealed to Israel for our ultimate benefit (Rom 15:4):

> Since the old covenant comes to an end on account of its darkness and imperfection, God has established, revealed and brought to light a covenant that is perfect, that abides unchanged throughout eternity (AIO 7.15).

Early Anabaptists quoted from the deuterocanonical works often and without distinguishing them from the Hebrew Bible, which suggests that they held to the Catholic and not the Protestant canon. Klaassen hypothesized that this might have been at least in part due to the fact that many Anabaptists used Zwingli's

Zürich Froschauer Bible, which integrated the deuterocanonicals into the Old Testament (AIO 7.0). The question of whether to include the deuterocanonical writings had been a live one within Roman Catholicism. It was finally settled at the Council of Trent (1563) in response to Protestant challenges to Roman Catholic authority.

Jesus As Hermeneutic Key

Anabaptists treat the New Testament as the hermeneutical key to understanding and applying the Old Testament. Early confessions affirm that "the Old Testament must be interpreted and reconciled according to the New Testament . . . and must be distinguished among the people of God" (33A).

Even greater than the New Testament, Jesus is the *eternal* Word of God, which must be distinguished from "the written Word of God, contained in the canonical books of the Holy Scriptures, which began in time, was revealed and given to us, and which in time shall end" (13A). Jesus thus has the authority to abrogate, revise, and reinterpret the Law of Moses. The Anabaptists pointed to the New Testament for proof of this. For example, Jesus "has entirely abolished and forbidden all aforementioned swearing of oaths" (33A), even though they were allowed in the Law of Moses. Regarding marriage, Jesus "the great Lawgiver of the New Testament established the original order" (CJC) of creation, setting aside Moses' allowance of divorce for reasons other than adultery:

> Christ, as a perfect law-giver (James 4:12), rejected and abolished the letter of divorce as a concession of Moses (Matt. 19:8), along with all abuses. And he pointed all his hearers and believers again to the first ordinance of his heavenly Father (made with Adam and Eve in Paradise) (33A).

This same principle of abrogating the Law of Moses in favor of something better was also applied to violence and warmaking. Grebel wrote, "Neither do [Christians] use worldly sword or war, since all killing has ceased with them—unless, indeed, we would still be of the old law" (AIO 13.1). Riedeman added:

> If one should say that David, who was loved by God, and other saints, went to war, and therefore one should still do so when one has right and justification thereto, we say, "No." That David and other saints did this, but that we ought not so to do, can be seen by all from the words quoted above, "To them of old is said, 'An eye for an eye and a tooth for a tooth,' but I say unto you, that ye resist not evil!" Here Christ makes the distinction himself. There is therefore no need for many words, for it is clear that Christians can neither go to war nor practise vengeance. Whosoever does this has forsaken and denied Christ and Christ's nature (AIO 13.14).

Distinguishing Between the Covenants

If this is so, then what place can the Old Testament, and particularly the Law of Moses, play in the lives of Christians? Early confessions affirm that "it is the word of command that was given to Moses at Mount Sinai, declaring to us the will of the most high" (WC) but that:

> Christ has brought to an end and removed from among his people the unbearable burden of the law of Moses . . . with its shadows and figures, the priestly office of the temple, altar, sacrifice and all else that was a part of the figurative priestly office—the kingly office and all that belonged to it: the kingdom, sword, law of revenge, war, and whatever prefigured his person and office . . . These were the image, the shadow of him who was to come (SC).

The Law of Moses was written particularly for Israel as a stipulation of their covenant with God and given "through the ministry of angels (John 1:17; Acts 7:53) as a perfect teaching and rule for the descendants of Abraham and Jacob (Gen. 17:2)" (33A). However, Jesus "cancelled the bond which pledged us to the decrees of the law" (DC) and "established a New Testament (Jer. 31:31), and hereto invited all heathens and peoples of the earth who were far-off strangers and enemies (Eph. 2:12), but are now all invited through [grace] (Rom. 4:17)" (33A).

Hutter cited additional support for this concept in Paul's letter to the Galatians: that "the law was [the Jews'] schoolmaster and they were imprisoned under external statutes until the time of Christ. He was to liberate those who were under the law so that they too would receive sonship" (AIO 12.9).

Thus, the Anabaptists have tended to emphasize discontinuity, rather than continuity, between the old and new covenants. Pilgram Marpeck, in his preface to the collective work *Explanation of the Testaments*, detailed a fairly standard viewpoint. In contrast to those who say that "Christ's suffering was retroactive to the Old Testament [and] actual forgiveness of sin in the Old Testament [led] to eternal life," Marpeck contended that "in the Old Testament it was all only fleshly, figurative, shadowy, and temporal," so that the "believers of the Old Testament hoped to receive [the things God promised] only when Christ became Man" (PM, VI. See also Col. 2:17 and Heb. 10:1, which he cites as biblical evidence for his position). For this reason Christ descended into hell, as the ancient creeds taught, "to preach the gospel to the dead and to the spirits in prison according to the Scriptures" (PM, VI).

The Hutterite theologian Peter Riedemann concurred that something new has come in Christ but nuanced this claim in an intriguing way. He saw the various covenants which God had made in biblical history as in some sense the same covenant, though with increasing brightness and clarity:

> God made his covenant first with Adam, and then more clearly with Abraham and his descendants . . . The old [Mosaic] covenant, insofar as it was called old, was given to the people of Israel without the dispensing of the Spirit of Grace . . . because sin was not taken from them . . . Although the old covenant brings bondage with it, yet it also ushers in something better and more perfect. Because something better has come, that is, the covenant of God is more perfectly and more clearly revealed, that

which is dark and imperfect must come to an end . . . This does not mean that God's covenant is finished and done with, but rather that the imperfect revelation of it is finished . . . This has been accomplished in Christ" (HCF).

Reflections

Anabaptism's centering of Jesus and the new covenant is consistent with New Testament theology and helps us to better discern how we are to live our lives today as Christians who imitate Christ. It also protects us against the idolatrous worship of the Bible which, though inspired by God, is not God.

One may see in early Anabaptism a hint of what would be developed in the Apocalyptic Paul school—that Jesus' incarnation had punctuated time to such a degree that what had come before had essentially come to an end in light of the newness that Christ had brought.

However, this centering of Jesus is not without its dangers if done out of balance, as Denck's abandonment of Scripture for spiritualism demonstrates. Schiemer's contention that "it is not really necessary" to read the Old Testament is wrongheaded on at least two counts:

1. Because it was inspired by God.

2. Because it was written for our instruction, as well as for its original audience.

We cannot properly understand the multifaceted work and nature of Christ if we ignore the Old Testament which prepared the way for him and provided the theological categories that he fulfilled. Contemporary scholarship, particularly the biblical theology movement and its popular expressions in resources like *The Bible Project,* has demonstrated the necessity of reading Jesus within the grand narrative of the whole of Scripture.

Early Anabaptists were having the right conversation about how to weigh and apply Scripture, but they didn't always come up with the right answers. In some forms of modern Anabaptism, this has led to a subjectivism and theological liberalism that threatens to cut itself off from not only the best early Anabaptist thinking but even historic, orthodox Christian thought as a whole.

2. God

WITH THE EXCEPTION OF some spiritualists and unitarians at the margins, Anabaptists held to an orthodox view of God as Trinity and of Christ as both God and man. However, some within mainstream Anabaptism did hold to a view of Christ's "heavenly body" which is not strictly orthodox and which will be described in more detail in our section about the nature of the Son. With that exception, much of what you would read from mainstream early Anabaptist confessions and theologians looks very much like what a faithful and knowledgeable Roman Catholic of Protestant Christian would affirm.

Trinity

In their confessions, the early Anabaptists affirm a belief in "the divine Trinity, Father, Son and Holy Spirit," and that "there is one single, eternal, omnipotent God" (CC). The three persons are "of one will, one mind, one essence, one Being, and therefore the only true, living, almighty, and eternal God" (WC). They "are neither divided nor different in nature, essence, or essential attributes" but are alike "eternal, omnipotent, invisible, immortal, glorious" (SC). Furthermore, "apart from this only God, there has never been, nor shall there be found any other eternally" (33A).

The orthodox doctrine of the Trinity which these confessions affirmed unites the Father, Son, and Spirit in nature but distinguishes them as persons. Thus, "what the Father does, the Son does as well" (33A), but also, "the Father (John 3:6; Rom. 8:3), in so far as he is Father, is other than the Son (John 16:28; Rom. 5:10), and the Son, insofar as he is the Son, is another from the Father and the Holy Spirit, and the Holy Spirit (John 14:16), insofar as he is the true Holy Spirit, is another from the Father and the Son" (CJC).

These early confessions also commonly affirm the *filioque*—the belief codified by the Western church, but denied by the East, that the Holy Spirit proceeds not only from the Father but also from the Son, an idea we will address in more detail in our section on the Holy Spirit:

> The Son is born and proceeds from the single, eternal being and substance of the Father. The Holy Spirit proceeds truly from the Father and Son, and is understood to be one, eternal, divine being with the Father and Son (33A).

The Nature of God

Early Anabaptist confessions likewise affirm orthodox understandings of the nature of God, as expressed in both the Eastern and Western church. There is

> one united, eternal and almighty God, who has neither beginning nor end, who fills all in heaven and earth and sustains all being, who is invisible and incomprehensible, to whom nothing is hidden, who knows the heart, desires and thoughts of all humans, who hears, knows and sees all things in heaven and earth, in the sea and under the earth . . . God [is] Lord and Creator of heaven and earth and of all that is in it, visible or invisible, also the sea and all flowing water, all living creatures in heaven and on earth, in the sea and under the earth. (CH).

He is not only eternal, omnipotent, and omniscient but "always perfect in love, longsuffering, gentle, kind, merciful, righteous and almighty, a fountain of life, from whom all good gifts flow" (WC).

The Anabaptists also affirmed the doctrine of aseity—that God "[exists] out of or through himself; having no need of any help or assistance from anything, but is himself the origin and fountain of all good things" (33A). This attribute of God is particularly emphasized by Reformed Christians, though in contradistinction to Reformed theology the Anabaptist God exists "without preferring one before the other, it is his desire that no one should be lost, and that all might be converted and become righteous" (WC).

Father

The Father is distinguished from the Son and the Holy Spirit both in eternity and in the functions which he performs for our sake within created time—and these aspects mirror one another. The Father "from eternity . . . brought forth his Son in an incomprehensible, and inexpressible manner" (WC), and therefore within time "Jesus Christ . . . was sent by God the Father from Heaven for our salvation" (CH). The reference to bringing forth from eternity refers to eternal generation, the act by which the Son, outside of space and time, is eternally begotten of the Father. Because of this begottenness, the Son is distinct from *the Father*. But because it happens in eternity, "before all creation," (SC), the Son is not a created being distinct from *God*. Indeed, the Son shares in the Father's divine nature and eternal existence:

> Jesus Christ, together with his human nature, is truly God, the Son of God from eternity, begotten of the Father, born out of him not in a manner which placed him outside of the Father as a separate Being, but being born from the Father in an inexpressible and incomprehensible manner he nevertheless remained in the Father (WC).

The contemporary Anglican theologian Kevin Giles highlights how, in Christian theology, the economic Trinity (the Trinity as it relates to creation) mirrors the Trinity in eternity: "The revelation of God's triunity in the economy (history) reflects accurately what is true of God in eternity."[1] Thus, the reason the Father sent the Son to save us (and not vice-versa) is because the Son was brought forth from the Father before creation—the Father sending forth the Son in time follows from the Father bringing forth the Son in eternity. The Anabaptists affirm this at least partly because the Nicene Creed affirmed it: "I believe in one Lord Jesus Christ, the Only Begotten Son of God, born of the Father before all ages."

In addition to being the source of the Son in eternity, the Father is also the ultimate source of all created things in time, through the work of the Son: "Through the Son the Father has created all things" (33A).

Son (Christology)

Christology can be divided into two parts—our theology of who the Son is by nature and the role he played in creation and in our salvation.

His Nature

The early Anabaptist confessions affirm both the full divinity and full humanity of Christ. The Son is "God of God, of divine being, like God in might, power, glory" but also "came into the flesh, was conceived by the Holy Spirit; took on the seed of Abraham according to the promise; became flesh in the virgin Mary through the power and work of the Holy Spirit" (CH). Thus the Son is "God and human in one person" (33A).

When he took on humanity, he did not cease to be divine. Instead, he added humanity to himself: "The eternal Son of God, remaining what he had been before, namely, God and Spirit, became that which he had formerly not been, namely, flesh or human" (SC). These natures did not combine to make some new third nature, but as Pilgram Marpeck wrote, "He is two natures, one Man, two natures, one God, divine and human in one" (AIO 1.7).

---

1. Giles, *Eternal Generation of the Son,* loc. 166.

As a true human,

> He experienced hunger (Matt. 4:2), thirst (John 19:28), fatigue from travel (John 4:6); he sighed (Mark 8:12), and wept (Luke 19:41) and grew in wisdom, maturity and grace with God and humanity (Luke 2:51) (33A).

However, early Anabaptists differed over what it meant for Jesus to be human. Dutch Anabaptist leaders like Menno Simons and Dirk Phillips held to the Melchiorite doctrine that Jesus' flesh did not derive from Mary but from heaven. This denial was meant to protect the perfection of Jesus and his perfect work on our behalf, "since a body made impure by sin could not be a perfect sacrifice for sins" (AIO 1).

As Melchior Hoffman wrote:

> Now if the body of Jesus Christ was . . . of Adam's flesh and blood as is openly affirmed, it follows that the redemption has not yet happened. For the seed of Adam belongs to Satan and is the property of the devil. Satan cannot be paid in his own coin . . . If it should be established that Christ's flesh was Mary's natural flesh and blood, we would all have to wait for another redeemer, for in such a one we could get no righteousness (AIO 1.5).

However, Anabaptists like Peter Riedeman denied the logic of Melchioritism, arguing that

> this Word proceeded from the Father that the harm brought by the transgression of Adam might be healed, and the fall restored; he took upon himself human nature and character, became man, became flesh, that even as through a man death came, even so resurrection from the dead and salvation might come through a man (AIO 1.6).

If we are indeed saved by our union with Jesus through his permanently taking on our humanity, then the idea that Christ's human nature is different from our own undermines the very ground of our salvation. As the early church father Gregory

Nazianzen famously wrote, "What has not been assumed has not been healed." While further reflections on Melchioritism will be offered at the end of this chapter, it is sufficient to say for now that this doctrine was a negative mark on an otherwise orthodox strain of Anabaptism, and its virtual disappearance from modern Anabaptism has been a positive development.

His Role

Jesus taking on humanity served a purpose within creation—the salvation of mankind through our union with him. When God the Son took on flesh, he bridged the gap between humanity and God—thus making possible our reunion with the divine. That's why Simons wrote that in Christ, the believer is "so united and mingled with God that he becomes a partaker of the divine nature and is made conformable to the image of his Son" (AIO 7.11).

Jesus coming in the flesh was in accordance with what was written in the Old Testament; thus he "is the true Messiah and champion, prophet and king, who was to come into the world, whom God had promised from the beginning in the Scriptures to the patriarchs" (CH). He did this to "save and free men and women from their sins, guilt, and unrighteousness and restore them again to God's favour" (DC).

Pilgram Marpeck stated simply of the Son's work that "forgiveness and remission of sins come alone through the Lord Jesus Christ" (AIO 1.8), while Peter Riedemann offered a slightly more expansive confession:

> The Lord Christ, the salvation of the world, was sent by the Father that those who believe on his name might have eternal life and be renewed into the divine likeness and grafted into his nature; which access to the Father and his grace he won through his death for us, who bear the likeness of his death (AIO 9.13).

Having completed the work of atonement on our behalf, "He shall live and reign as a ruling (Luke 1:29; Ps. 45:7) king of all kings and lord of all lords over Mount Zion and the house of Jacob (Rev. 19:16). And he shall reign forever and ever" (33A).

Holy Spirit (Pneumatology)

The third person of the Trinity is often overlooked in Christian theologizing, though this is less so in charismatic and mystically oriented communities. Of course, early Anabaptism also had its mystical side. While modern Anabaptism has been stereotyped as rigidly moralistic and suspicious of the mystical, a number of early Anabaptist groups emphasized the "inner word" of God's speaking to their hearts to an even greater degree than the "outer word" of God's witness in the Holy Scriptures. However, in the early Anabaptist confessions we find the Holy Spirit spoken of in fairly traditional western Christian language.

His Nature

Anabaptist confessions of the first hundred and fifty years or so spoke of the Holy Spirit in language that could be affirmed by Catholic and Protestant Christians alike, though not as consistently by the Eastern Orthodox. They affirmed with all Christians that the Holy Spirit "is of one essence with the Father and the Son" (WC). They ascribed to him divine qualities and called him "true God (Acts 5:4 and 17:28) with the Father and Son" (33A). However, in opposition to the Eastern Orthodox they confessed "also that though this Spirit is of one essence with the Father and the Son, undivided, he nevertheless proceeds from the Father *and the Son*" (WC, emphasis added).

The Anabaptists' confession that "the Holy Spirit [proceeds] from the Father and the Son" (SC) situated them firmly within the Western Christian tradition, and here's why.

The Nicene-Constantinopolitan Creed, which had been affirmed by both Eastern and Western Christians as a basic and universal statement of Christian belief, had it that the Holy Spirit proceeded from the Father in a fashion similar to the eternal generation of the Son (see the previous section on the Son). Over time, however, the Western churches became convinced that the Holy Spirit *also* proceeded from the Son. This conclusion was reached largely from the Bible's statements that the Holy Spirit had been sent by *both* the Father and the Son to his people (John 15:26, 16:7), and the logic of this procession in time suggested to them a procession from Father and Son in eternity similar to the Father's eternal generation of the Son. Perhaps the Eastern churches could have treated this as an "agree to disagree" issue, but the Western church's unilateral addition of *filioque* (a Latin word meaning "and the Son") to a creed which had been crafted to represent the unity of the *entire* church was too much for Eastern Christians. The *filioque* controversy was a key issue which eventually led to the separation of Christendom into two distinct domains—the Eastern Orthodox and the Roman Catholic. Early Anabaptist confessions and leaders like Peter Riedemann affirmed the Western formulation of the creed; perhaps because they thought it was superior to the Eastern, or perhaps simply because it was the formulation which they had received as Western Christians:

> But as the Son or the Word proceeds from the Father and yet remains in him, the Holy Spirit proceeds from them both and remains in them both for ever and ever (AIO 3.8).

His Role

Regardless of whether or not the Holy Spirit also proceeds from the Son in eternity, the Scriptures and the Anabaptist confessions certainly testify that he is sent by the Son to the church and that it is the Holy Spirit "through whom the Father and Son work (Ps. 33:6) and through whom heaven and earth, with all the heavenly hosts, have been created and made." (33A).

The Holy Spirit is God at his nearest to us because he "enlightens the hearts of people" (33A) and "is sent by the Father to all believers to [give] strength and consolation and constance in all tribulation until the end" (SA). Indeed, the Holy Spirit is the direct agent of salvation for each individual:

> He is given by God to all who are obedient to him (Acts 5:32). All who are driven by this Spirit are God's children (Rom. 8:9, 14). Whoever does not have this Spirit does not belong to God. [The Holy Spirit] is called the seal and pledge of the inheritance of all true children of God (Eph. 1:14 and 4:30). Whoever blasphemes this Spirit can expect no forgiveness for eternity (Matt. 12:31). It is commanded by Christ to baptize believers also in his name (Matt. 28:19) (33A).

The Hutterite theologian Peter Riedemann wrote that "in the Holy Spirit we have all comfort, delight and fruitfulness" because he

> teaches, directs and instructs us, assures us that we are children of God, and makes us one with God, so that through his working we thus become incorporated into and partakers of the divine nature and character (AIO 3.8).

Dirk Philips concurred, speaking of the Spirit's essential role in our salvation and his intermediary role on behalf of the Father and the Son:

> By him they are enlightened, renewed and sanctified (Tit. 3:6; 1 Cor. 3:11), and become a possession of God (Eph. 1:14) and new creatures in Christ. By him they are kept to everlasting life, and without him no one knows God or believes in Jesus Christ (AIO 3.11).

Other Spiritual Beings

While the early Anabaptist confessions did not give much attention to spiritual beings like angels and demons, other Anabaptist writers did give us material which we can appeal to in order to fill out the Anabaptist worldview regarding the spiritual realm.

Angels (Angelology)

Perhaps borne out of a desire to avoid the perceived excesses in Catholicism regarding the veneration of angels and saints, early Anabaptist confessions spend almost no time on angelology. Among Anabaptist leaders, however, one interesting idea about angels is attested to: that the church encompasses more than just humans grafted into Christ but also angelic beings. As Dirk Philips wrote:

> The church of God was originally begun by God in heaven with the angels, who were created spirits and flaming fire (Ps. 104:4; Heb. 1:7), to stand before the throne of God praising and serving him" (AIO 5.10).

This idea presents the church as a family of spiritual beings which humans are invited to join. We have here, in seed form at least, a concept which has been developed (and at times overdeveloped) in more mystical strains of Christianity, as well as in modern biblical theology's explication of the Bible's "divine council" teaching and the future role that Christians will have in it.

Satan and the Demons (Demonology)

The confessions give a bit more attention to the infernal side of angelology—demonology. In particular, Satan is described in his role as adversary, tempter, and the ultimate source of oppression against Anabaptist Christians by their Protestant and Catholic contemporaries.

In the broad view:

> There is a visible, perishable kingdom of this world (Matt. 4:8), which through the sins and evil of humanity is covered in darkness (John 5:19), where Satan and the spirit of evil (Eph. 2:2, 6:12) (which works among the children of disbelief) is the supreme prince of this darkness, who at the end, with all his servants, shall be moved to an eternal cry where he will mourn and perish (33A).

Satan's persecution of the Anabaptists was only the latest in a longstanding campaign to oppose God's purposes: "Through the Devil's envy (Wis. 2:24) and the sin of our first parents (Rom. 5:12; 1 Cor. 15:21; Gen. 3:6), death has come into the world" (33A). Our parents' sin was not distinct from the work of Satan, but the result of his scheming: "The devil has turned us aside, so that he might destroy and cast down the work of God" (SA).

Thankfully, Christ has "crushed the serpent's head, that is, robbed the devil of his power and dominion" (LLF), thus giving the decisive blow to Satan. However, this victory is not applied to each person until they turn to Christ: "Christ has overcome the devil in [each Christian] too, has torn away his snare (his sin), set him free, and reconciled him with God" (HCF).

Though beaten, Satan has not yet been totally neutralized. God "can redeem and eternally save us from the captivity of sin (2 Tim. 2:26), hell (1 Cor. 15:55), the devil and death" (33A), but this work will not be fully done until the return of Christ. In the meantime, he "arms [us] with spiritual weapons for a spiritual warfare against all [our] enemies, the spirits of evil under heaven with their associates upon earth (John 10:28; Matt. 23:36; 2 Cor. 10:4; Eph. 6: 17,13)" (33A). Thus the infernal spirits "fear him and tremble in his presence. He has overcome them, bound them, and taken away their power. Christ has delivered us, their prey, who were held captive in death, and set us free" (HCF).

As we await the final judgment, we must fight the evil ones in the spiritual plane, not the physical one. To his people, Jesus

> has taught against and forbidden all vengeance (whether by words or works) (Matt. 20:25; Rom. 12:19; 1 Pet. 3:9), and has ordered them to [follow] his own example to be armed only with the armour of God and the sword of the spirit (which is God's word) (Eph. 6:13; 2 Cor. 10:4), in order to fight against flesh and blood, world and sin (1 John 5:4), and the manifold attacks of the Devil (2 Tim. 4:7)" (33A).

There is a hint in these words that the kingdoms of men might be closely connected and empowered by the kingdom of

Satan, though this idea is left tantalizingly underdeveloped in the major Anabaptist confessional works. More on that later.

Humans (Anthropology)

Anabaptists also held that humans are spiritual beings

> consisting of body and soul, of soul and body. The soul is not the essence of the body, nor is the body the essence of the soul. The body is the house, temple, or tabernacle in which the soul lives, but the soul is the spirit dwelling in the body, the natural life and ruler, which the Scriptures in various places call spirit, breath, or life. Even as every person has only one body, so also every person has one soul, the two together united, body and soul, making the person complete (WC).

One confession notes that "this only God created humans good (Gen. 1:31) in his own image and likeness (Gen. 1:27)" (SC). Another adds:

> He gifted them with wisdom, speech and reason, so that they could know, fear, serve, love and be obedient to their Creator; being so regarded and chosen that they should always live for him (Wis. 2:23 and 1:14), governing and ruling over all creatures which God the Lord had made (Gen. 1:26) (33A).

Riedemann likewise testified to the doctrine that God created us to rule with him: "When God made them to rule over all creatures, he explained to them that as they were lords over the creatures, God was Lord over them" (LLF). Elsewhere he wrote: "[God] made heaven his throne but gave the earth with all that adorns it to people, making them rulers over it so that they might learn to know the Creator and Overseer" (HCF).

But something went wrong with this perfect order: "Humanity has lost the image of God in him, and through the gifts of evil, God himself" (WC). Thus "man is by nature inclined to do evil from his youth and is prone to sin and wickedness" (DC). However, more so than their Lutheran and Reformed contemporaries, the early Anabaptists taught that a divine spark still remained in man:

> Yet we confess that this same human being has not been robbed completely of the image and light of God, else he would have become complete darkness even as the devils are. We confess, however, that in his mercy, God left a trace of light in fallen humanity and its descendants. Through this it is still able to achieve some virtues and avoid some sins, and can, through trust and the grace of God, come to a closer walk [with God] (WC).

Since "this ability to accept or reject the grace of God has remained with the posterity of the first humans as a gift of grace," (SC) "they are able to accept or reject the bountiful grace of God" (33A). In short, humans maintain a freedom of the will, which, though twisted, enables us to respond to God's grace.

This doctrine of a prevenient grace which enables all human beings to come to God seemed quite logical and even obvious to the Anabaptists, even if it was not so obvious to the Reformers. One confession contends that God giving humans the ability to respond to his gracious overtures "was fitting so that he could be a just judge and have proper reasons to punish his despisers with the pains of hell" (CJC). Another asks rhetorically, "Would he threaten to punish them with the eternal death and damnation if they could desire only those things they were forced to [accept]?" (33A).

Another issue regarding human nature has to do with whether we were created immortal. Despite Edward Fudge's claim that "many Anabaptists held conditionalist views about final punishment,"[2] the major Anabaptists confessions took a decidedly traditionalist view regarding the immortality of the human soul. The Waterlander Confession, for instance, states that "though the body loses its natural life when the soul departs, the body being under [the judgment of] death, the soul, nevertheless, retains the power of life, being imperishable and immortal" (WC).

---

2. Fudge, *Fire That Consumes*, 312

This confession is representative in that it also presents a fairly traditional view regarding the intermediate state between death and resurrection:

> We believe that the souls of believers, after being separated from the body in death, are carried by angels to places where they taste and feel joy and happiness… [and] contrariwise, that the souls of unbelievers, after being separated from the body in death, are carried [to places] where they suffer pain and fear (WC).

However, there is evidence of some diversity among Anabaptists regarding the intermediate state. In particular, the Thirty Three Articles promotes the notion of "soul sleep"—that between death and resurrection the soul is either nonexistent or unconscious.

At times, these articles appear to be supporting Fudge's view of conditional immortality, contending that Adam and Eve "fell through sin into the wrath and disfavour of God, and on the same day became subject to temporal and eternal death" and thus "return to the earth (as a wage of sin) (Gen. 3:19; Rom. 6:23; Gen. 2:17) from which they came" (33A).

But all becomes clear when this Dutch Mennonite confession states directly its position on soul sleep:

> Seeing that in the scriptures the natural death is called a sleep (1 Cor. 15:6; Matt. 9:24) and the resurrection of the dead an awakening from this sleep of death (John 11:11; Dan. 12:13), and just as a sleeping person can receive and use neither for his soul nor his body any good gifts, much less any punishment, pain and torment until he has been first awakened from his sleep (Gen. 40:5), in this way believers cannot receive the perfect heavenly nature, nor the unbelievers the eternal death or pain of hell, neither in the soul nor the body, until they have been first awakened and raised up from this sleep of death through the coming of Christ" (33A).

Reflections

The Forgotten Holy Spirit

There should never be a contradiction between the "inner word" and the "outer word" of God, since the same Holy Spirit speaks both in our hearts and in Scripture. But there is an equal and opposite danger which must also be avoided—the danger of displacing the Holy Spirit's work in our hearts to opt instead for an emphasis on conformity to community rules. Though codes of behavior are not necessarily a bad thing, they should never replace the reality of the Holy Spirit living inside of us. As Peter Riedemann wrote:

> We believe that in the Holy Spirit we have all comfort, delight and fruitfulness and that he confirms, brings to pass, carries out and perfects all things; that he also teaches, directs and instructs us, assures us that we are children of God, and makes us one with God, so that through his working we thus become incorporated into and partakers of the divine nature and character (AIO 3.8).

Here the Spirit is described in terms that are very personal. This is appropriate since he is meant to be quite close to us; indeed he is meant to be in us and part of us. No mere community code of ethics can replace that reality.

Ruling with God

The notion of mankind being created to rule alongside God is not strongly attested to in the confessions, though occasional references to it can be found in other Anabaptist writings. In contrast, some strains of Reformed Christianity developed from this doctrine the view that Christians, now restored in Christ, have inherited the earth and fully possess it. The modern Christian Nationalist theorist Stephen Wolfe quotes Calvin approvingly on this point:

> And since all things are subject to Christ, we are fully restored by His mediation, and that through faith; and

therefore all that unbelievers enjoy may be regarded as the property of others, which they rob or steal... our disposition toward all good things, even those possessed by unbelievers, should be informed by the fact that they are ours in Christ.[3]

In short, the world and all the things which unbelievers possess actually belong to true Christians. If this is so, then it is proper for Christians to behave as the world's rightful rulers. No wonder the lives and property of Anabaptists were treated as forfeit by the Protestants!

Did Anabaptists underemphasize man's initial co-rulership with God because this mindset was being used to justify the theft and murder of their own people by those claiming to be the only true heirs of God? Perhaps. But Anabaptists should not fear the proper use of the doctrine of our co-rulership with God. Instead, we should develop it from our own tradition's sensitivities to biblical teaching which has often been neglected by traditional Protestant and Catholic theologians.

Pilgram Marpeck gives us a starting point when he contrasts the "kingdom of earth" which seeks to "rule over man" now with the proper biblical timeline: "With Christ in patience, man is lord of the whole earth" (AIO 6.14). Hutter adds that not now, but in the eschaton, "the godly will rule and reign" (AIO 17.10).

From an Anabaptist perspective, ruling with Christ is not only a question of when, but how. Calvin's understanding of ruling seems to be rooted in a worldly, carnal understanding of the word. However, early Anabaptists appealed to this passage to discern what it meant to be powerful as followers of Jesus:

> You know that the rulers of the Gentiles lord it over them, and their high officials exercise authority over them. Not so with you. Instead, whoever wants to become great among you must be your servant, and whoever wants to be first must be your slave—just as the Son of Man did not come to be served, but to serve, and to give his life as a ransom for many (Matt 20:25–28 NIV).

3. Wolfe, *Case for Christian Nationalism*, 114–15.

Citizens of God's kingdom are marked by nonviolence and our adherence to the Sermon On The Mount, which is antithetical to the kinds of oppressive human rule which mark the kingdoms of men.

The Kingdoms of Men, the Kingdom of Satan

A related area for growth in Anabaptist thought has to do with our understanding of Satan's influence over human government. More will be said on this in our reflections on holy living.

3. Salvation (Soteriology)

UNDER THE HEADING OF salvation, we have included the Anabaptist doctrines of sin, the church, and ethics. The reason for this is that in Anabaptist thought, we are saved *from* sin *for* the purpose of Christian community and obedience to God.

Anabaptists have been accused by some Protestants of holding to salvation by works. As we survey the more nuanced approaches to grace, faith, and works presented by the early Anabaptists, we should keep in mind Menno Simons' words about the grace of God:

> If God should judge us according to our deserts and not according to His great goodness and mercy, then I confess with the holy David that no man could stand before His judgment... Therefore it should be far from us that we should comfort ourselves with anything but the grace of God through Christ Jesus... We do not believe nor teach that we are to be saved by our merits and works as the envious assert without truth. We are to be saved solely by grace through Christ Jesus (CDS).

Saved by...

Christ's Work

Early Anabaptists were quick to emphasize that no salvation was possible without the work of Christ. Marpeck wrote, mirroring the Reformation doctrine of *Solus Christus*, that "forgiveness and remission of sins come alone through the Lord Jesus Christ" (AIO 1.8). The confessions spoke of "the atonement of the blood of Christ Jesus" (SA), which is the the doctrine that "Christ gave His life for us, and shed His blood for us" (CO). As our substitute, the innocent Christ "has taken all of our guilt upon himself" (33A). However, Anabaptists tended to emphasize, more so than many Protestants, that salvation is not just being delivered from hell at the moment that one first believes, but the placement of one's whole self *into* Christ and all that flows from that union.

Thus, Riedemann pointed to Christ as the guarantor of every part of our salvation:

> Christ leads us to be partakers of his nature, character, and being. This is a goodness that saves and leads to God. Christ is our righteousness and goodness. He is our life; we ourselves do not live, but Christ lives in us. Christ is our resurrection, our salvation, and our all in all. We also believe that Christ's incarnation means that we can be transformed. His suffering and death are salvation and life for us. In Christ we truly have everything (HCF).

Like the Protestant reformers, Anabaptists critiqued the Catholic mass for implying that Christ's work was not final and sufficient because he "must suffer and be sacrificed every day," in opposition to the New Testament "teaching that Christ has perfected all who should be sanctified by a single offering, and that he himself has sat down at the right hand of God's throne and is sacrificed no more" (LLF).

However, one distinct emphasis of Anabaptist soteriology is that they took pains to underline that Christ's work was not accomplished by exercising violence upon others, but by taking it upon himself:

> Since his kingdom was not of this world (John 18:36), he also did not enter upon it with physical weapons of iron or steel (Matt. 4:1; Luke 4:1; Mark 16:21) but through suffering and struggling in the flesh, preparing for him purification through temptation, distress and suffering,

and treading the cursed death (Gal. 3:13; Deut. 21:13)
on the cross under Pontius Pilate (I Tim. 6:13)" (CJC).[1]

Some modern Anabaptists have sought to expand their doctrine of nonviolence by removing all violent intent from the person of God. As a result, they have abandoned the doctrine that Christ's blood propitiates God's enmity against us. However, their forebears were not so squeamish about blood atonement making us right with God. One confession speaks of our being "reconciled with God and [thus we] are at peace, having a certain high hope and assurance of entry into eternal life" on account of Christ's "unique sacrifice upon the cross" (SC). Another uses the language of "ransom" often picked up by ransom theory atonement proponents, but places it alongside theological statements of "payment for the sins of the world" and "reconciliation for the sins of the world before the Father" (13A). Yet another proclaims that "we are reconciled with God (Rom. 8:22, 5:10) through the blood and death of his Son who accomplished the cleansing of our sins in himself (Heb. 1:3)" (CJC).

However, despite their agreement with Reformed teaching on this aspect of soteriology, they departed from their Reformed contemporaries by seeing the atonement of Christ as "a universal offering" (SC) that was unlimited in scope—available to all who freely believe in him; not only to those individuals whom Calvin taught had been selected for salvation by God's eternal decree.

They also expanded God's grace to children who could not yet believe. The Swiss Brethren Confession of Hesse is fairly representative:

> Children are blessed [or saved] because of the promise as long as they remain innocent and cannot yet distinguish between good and evil. As for [Adam's sin], it is not accounted to them, even though they are of a sinful disposition, because through the death of Christ and through Christ's shed blood they are reconciled (CH).

1. There is a similar idea expressed by Martin Luther in his dichotomy of the theology of the cross and the theology of glory, though his concept was broader and more spiritual—and it did not lead him to reject violence.

In his 1532 Confession, Pilgram Marpeck expanded on the Anabaptist rationale for seeing unbaptized children as protected by God's grace. Firstly, while humanity has a sinful nature, "the guilt of sin consists of knowledge," meaning that "those who are... baptized must be persons who have recognized their sin and inability in the law, just as the ancients and those who knew the law." Since children and the severely mentally handicapped do not have this knowledge, they are in a sense innocent. Thus Marpeck argues that "innocent children cannot accept Christ; rather, Christ has accepted them as children in His kingdom" on the basis that Jesus said of children, "for to such belongs the kingdom of God" (PM, III. See also Luke 18:16).

Marpeck went on to argue that infant baptism subverted the consistent pattern of the teaching of the New Testament: "According to the word of Paul, we can sacrifice only ourselves and not someone else: 'Give your own bodies...' He does not add: 'and your children, as a sacrifice.'" Why? Because

> no one can have faith for anyone else, neither wife for husband, husband for wife, children for parents, nor parents for children, but everyone will believe or disbelieve, be saved or condemned for himself (PM, III).

In short, Christ's work under normal conditions must be applied to the individual by faith, but it is powerful enough—and God is gracious enough—to apply it even when faith is not present because the individual is not mentally competent to exercise faith.

More than one early Anabaptist source speaks of the harrowing of hell—the belief that Jesus, prior to his resurrection, descended to the place of the dead and proclaimed the gospel to Old Testament believers in order to give them an opportunity to repent, believe, and be released. The inclusion of this idea in so many Anabaptist confessions and writings is at least partially the result of many of these confessions being modeled after the early Christian creeds which included the sentence "he descended into hell." To give one representative example:

> We believe, acknowledge and confess that Jesus Christ, God's Son, our Lord and Saviour, through divine power descended into hell and redeemed the souls of the believing Old Testament patriarchs (CH).

However, this doctrine was also important because it supported the Anabaptist contention that in Christ salvation had truly been revealed—a salvation which was not yet available to old covenant believers in its fullness. Peter Riedemann explains:

> That he might fulfill all things, we confess that he also went down to the lowest parts of the earth (namely to the place of captivity, where they are kept who aforetime believed not the word which was spoken to them) and proclaimed to the spirits in prison that the word of salvation had now been sent, which had previously been resolved upon by God and promised to men, that all who believe it wholeheartedly might thereby be set free; and that he had now, in accordance with the promise given to the fathers, destroyed the power of death, hell and the devil, which had for so long betrayed and deceived them (AIO 4.13).

To this we can add Marpeck:

> The faith of the ancients was not sufficient for the sonship of the Spirit. Such power first came through Christ.

Thus, before Jesus' death,

> all were shackled, bound, and imprisoned until the time of the Son of God, who Himself preached the gospel to them in the lowest places of the earth (PM, III).

While the precise meaning of Peter's claim that Jesus proclaimed to the spirits in prison (1 Pet 3:18–20) is still debated amongst theologians, the common early Anabaptist reading was useful because it strengthened their conviction that something momentous had happened in Christ's coming which separated the church of Christ from what had come before.

While we will discuss what we are saved *for* in a later section, a brief sampling here of what Christ's work accomplished will suffice:

> The Lord Christ bought them with his costly blood (Acts 20:28), and washed and cleansed them with the water of the Holy Spirit (Eph. 5:26), in order that he could present them an honourable church without spot or wrinkle or the like (CJC).

> The Lord Christ, the salvation of the world, was sent by the Father that those who believe on his name might have eternal life and be renewed into the divine likeness and grafted into his nature; which access to the Father and his grace he won through his death for us, who bear the likeness of his death (Riedemann, AIO 9.13).

> And this same one will tread on the head of the serpent and thus take away the power of Satan (Heb. 2:14; 2 Tim. 1:10; 1 Cor. 15:4), and thereby deliver the whole human race from the wrath of God and from eternal death (33A).

Now that the work of atonement has been completed once and for all, "Jesus Christ, God's Son, our Lord and Saviour, ascended into heaven and is seated at the right hand of God, the almighty Father" (CH). Therefore, we wait patiently for when Jesus "will come again on the last day to judge the living and the dead" (CH).

God's Plan

Anabaptists conceived of God's plan and purpose in ways very different from Reformed Christians but still well within the realm of Christian orthodoxy. Whereas Reformed Christians seek to protect God's *sovereignty* by crediting him with all which comes to pass, Anabaptists look to protect his *character* as a loving Father by denying his hand in any kind of sin or evil which might take place on the earth. Since God is "perfectly good and love itself," he "desired the best for his creatures, namely, healing and salvation.

Therefore he neither predestined, determined, nor created anyone for damnation" (SC). Moreover:

> Whatever appears before God as presumptuous, as a departure from his commandment—all disobedience, all sin, all malice and evil brought forth among people—is neither contrary nor in accordance with his will, work or order, though he patiently sees and allows it. In summary, we confess that God at times punishes people because of his righteousness. This punishment, though it seems evil to human eyes, is righteous before God. Therefore he also orders, and brings to a good end, the evil works of the godless (WC).

While Reformed Christians see salvation as only for those individuals whom God foreordained it, Anabaptists

> believe that in Adam God created all people for salvation and eternal life, but because of their fall, and departure from eternal good and life, God foreordained his Son from the beginning as the mercy seat, sending him in the form of a servant when the time was fulfilled (WC).

In God's plan, salvation is offered to any and all comers because "without preferring one before the other, it is his desire that no one should be lost, and that all might be converted and become righteous" (WC).

Nevertheless, like the Reformed, Anabaptists likewise acknowledge humanity's "helplessness to save themselves" (DC) because through Adam's sin,

> they fell so deeply, became estranged and separated from God, that neither they themselves, nor any of their posterity, nor angels, nor any other creature in heaven or earth could help them, redeem them, or reconcile them to God. They would have been eternally lost had not God in compassion for his creatures intervened in his love and mercy (DC).

Thus, God's salvation plan makes our redemption and reconciliation possible.

Despite the old covenant given to Israel through Moses pre-dating the gospel of Jesus Christ in its revelation, the so-called "new covenant" predates the old in the plan and purpose of God. The Mosaic covenant was temporary and thus came "to an end because of its obscurity and imperfection," but "God has established a perfect covenant and revealed it to us. This covenant remains unchanged through eternity" (HCF, appealing to Jer 31:31–34). In other words, God's plan was to create a people for himself and sin did not prevent this plan from coming to pass.

The Spirit's Intercession

While God's plan and Christ's work make our salvation possible, it must be applied through the work of the Holy Spirit:

> We are pardoned of all past and present sins through the shed blood of Jesus Christ, receiving the true righteousness which he pours out richly upon us in co-operation with the Holy Spirit (SC).

Indeed, one becomes a Christian when "through God's Word and the Holy Spirit [they] are born again from above" (CH). "God gathers his church through his Spirit. The church cannot be gathered in any other way" (HCF).

For this reason, Riedemann speaks of the Holy Spirit's work as essential and necessary for salvation:

> The children of God, however, become his children through the unifying Spirit. Thus, it is evident that the church is gathered together by the Holy Spirit: also that she has being and is kept in being by him, and that there is no other church apart from that which the Holy Spirit builds and gathers (AIO 5.9).

Our Faith

Early Anabaptists affirmed faith as the gateway to individual salvation, that "one must necessarily believe in this one God… in order to be saved" (33A). Simons is clear that this faith is necessary for salvation but not meritorious:

> By faith they are born of him. He forgives them all their sins; has compassion on all their human shortcomings and weaknesses… And this we say, not by our own merits and works, but by grace through Christ Jesus (AIO 2.27).

However, just as faith is necessary to receive this salvation, it is also necessary to maintain it. The Anabaptists noticed that in the Scriptures, some Christians who once believed and tasted God's grace eventually fell away (Heb 3:6, 6:4–5). Other Scriptures highlighted a future judgment of works which applied even to confessing Christians to verify that they were truly in the faith (Rom 2:5–7; 2 Cor 5:10; 1 Pet 1:17; Gal 6:8). Moreover, since in the New Testament good works are expected and mark the sincere Christian, they cannot be totally distinguished from faith, as if it could be alone (Matt 7:15–20; Gal 6:15).

Protestants resolved this tension by arguing that works do flow from true faith, but nevertheless faith and works must be carefully separated to avoid the doctrine of salvation by works. Anabaptists reconciled the tensions between faith and works in a distinct but not altogether different way. They described saving faith as that faith which does not do "works which are accomplished outside of faith and the love of God… in order that [we] might thereby be justified" but rather a saving faith produces "works of faith" (LMS 7). These are not works done under our own power but are works "of God and Christ" through us (LMS 7). Riedemann thus acknowledged that

> faith is God's gift, and given to men that they might thereby seek and find God; who, when he has been found, stirs up and works all things in them through faith, so that in believers, in proportion to their faith,

nothing takes place save what God works in men, as Paul says, "Not I, but the grace of God," and again, "Not I live now, but Christ lives in me" (AIO 2.24).

Since faith is "not a human attribute" but "a gift from God, given only to those who fear God," it "is truly a power of God, renewing people and making them resemble God in his nature, living in God's righteousness, ardent in God's love, and observing his commandments" (HCF).

Therefore, since works done through us by God cannot be separated from sincere faith, Hubmaier concluded:

Faith alone and by itself is not sufficient for salvation… Now we do not wish to be mouth Christians only, to boast and say: O yes, we believe that Jesus Christ suffered agony and death for us. Rather, faith must express itself also in love to God and the neighbor.

Mocking Protestants for encouraging what he saw as moral laxness, Hubmaier went on:

O, we wish to be good evangelical Christians; we boast about our great faith, but have never touched the works of the gospel and faith with the smallest finger. Therefore we are, as stated above, nothing but mouth Christians, ear Christians, and paper Christians, but not action Christians (AIO 2.2).

Riedemann also lent his support to this understanding of "works of faith," writing that

the person in whom Christ is to become victorious must wholeheartedly surrender himself to Christ. That person must stand firm and allow Christ's work to be done in him. However, when this does not happen, Christ does not work in a person, and such a person remains in sin forever (HCF).

A tract sometimes attributed to Michael Sattler reasons in a similar vein, asking, "How could God have pleasure in one who either would not want to hear the will of God… or having heard it and known it would hold to it only verbally" (LMS 7)? To this rhetorical question even most Protestants would give a hearty amen. The tract further elaborates:

> For although He is truly a reconciliation for the whole world, nevertheless this does not benefit anyone, except only those who recognize and accept Him, through faith. Those, however, who do this, keep the command of Christ. He who does not do this and still boasts of Christ as his reconciliation, he is a liar, for he has not yet ever known Christ, as John testifies (LMS 7).

However, many of the same Protestants who would applaud Sattler's question would be less likely to give an amen to Menno Simon's critique due to its chastising Luther's movement by name:

> The Lutherans teach and believe that faith alone saves, without any assistance by works. They emphasize this doctrine so as to make it appear as though works were not even necessary; yes, that faith is of such a nature that it cannot tolerate any works alongside of it. And therefore the important and earnest epistle of James (because he reproves such a frivolous, vain doctrine and faith) is esteemed and treated as a "strawy epistle." What bold folly (TCF)!

To be clear, saving faith "is not an empty or hidden thing born within humans" but "true, upright faith... comes from God" (33A). Nevertheless, it does require cooperation and perseverance on our parts: "If we believe in him and remain in his Word, we will be his true disciples and recognize the truth, and through such faith we will inherit eternal life" (CH). For the early Anabaptists, faith was not something exercised at an initial moment in time but ongoing and a way of life.

This faith is also inextricably tied to repentance, which is a change of mind and a commitment to change one's behavior in accordance with love of God and neighbor:

> We believe, acknowledge and confess that whoever wants to come to God and become a partaker of his heavenly kingdom, of his grace and Holy Spirit, must recognize and confess his sin and die to the same; turn to God

with a repentant life, believe in Christ and be renewed through the Gospel (CH).

Indeed, when we first believe "we are truly justified… we are pardoned of all past and present sins through the shed blood of Jesus Christ, receiving the true righteousness which he pours out richly upon us in co-operation with the Holy Spirit," but it doesn't end there. Through our cooperation with the Holy Spirit, "we are transformed from being evil to being good, from a carnal state to a spiritual state, from selfishness to mildness, from pride to humility, being changed from unrighteousness to righteousness (Titus 3:5–6; 1 Cor 6:12). This justification flows from the rebirth" (SC). Riedemann summarizes:

> Love flows from faith; for where there is no faith there cannot be love, and where there is no love there cannot be faith. The two are so entwined that one cannot be pleasing to God without the other (LLF).

Faith works through love. If it does not, one may justly ask whether faith exists at all.

Reflections

Faith or Works?

Anabaptist thought regarding what saves us—faith or works—exposes a paradox which warrants further exploration.

Reformed Christians in the tradition of John Calvin hold that God saves us monergistically, which is to say without any effort on our part. In short, God predestines some to salvation and others to damnation. As a result of God justifying us without any effort on our part, he also gives us the Holy Spirit, which sanctifies us and changes our behavior—though in Reformed thought sin remains a significant and ongoing problem to overcome in the lives of believers.

But many Protestants after Arminius, and especially after Wesley, do not affirm this monergistic model of salvation. Instead, they argue that our faith and our will is free. But if we do not will to do any good works after we believe, are we truly saved? Some free will proponents who advocate eternal security (also known as "once saved, always saved" theology) double down on salvation by faith alone, affirming that good works are expected, but they are not actually necessary in the life of a Christian once faith has been asserted. While this view has become popular in some circles, even many Protestants who believe in *sola fide* (faith alone) see this perspective as heretical. This kind of faith is not a sincere faith which works but a passive belief, which, once asserted, does its magic permanently.

Modern evangelical scholarship has (perhaps unintentionally) followed the 16th-century Anabaptists in interrogating this understanding of faith as passive belief, with the result that a number of Protestant scholars have begun to suggest different understandings of the Greek word *pistis*, which our English Bibles translate as "faith." Matthew Bates, for example, in his book *Salvation by Allegiance Alone*, has highlighted ancient Greek uses of the word *pistis* which point to social, political, and military allegiances, arguing that a faith which saves us may be more like allegiance than belief. Perhaps more helpfully, Nijay Gupta's *Paul and the Language of Faith* highlights a spectrum of meaning for *pistis* contemporaneous with the New Testament ranging between faithfulness and belief, with trust as the central idea. The distinction between faith and trust is subtle but significant. While the word *faith* tends to suggest something passive, *trust* is more dynamic. It is a belief, an attitude, an orientation, but it also results in changed behavior—though not necessarily perfectly changed behavior. To trust someone is an inward disposition toward them which causes us to *behave* as if they can be counted on, so that we can confidently do what they ask of us believing that we will not regret our obedience.

Protestants have rightly taught that at the moment when we first trusted, we crossed over from death to life. However, our works count as evidence of whether this trust is real and ongoing, which is why God will judge us by them.

Anabaptists preceded many of the conclusions of these modern scholars and largely settled these debates for themselves nearly five hundred years ago. Nevertheless there is a danger here to avoid—both the early Anabaptists and those who are persuaded by the conclusions of modern scholars like Bates and Gupta may flirt with works salvation—the idea that we are saved by our own efforts and not by trusting in the work of Christ on our behalf.

At its best, early Anabaptism retrieved the biblical emphasis of grace working through faith to produce good works—in opposition to Catholicism and Protestantism, which tended to unhelpfully divide and emphasize one over the other. However, not all early Anabaptists emphasized the grace of God in full biblical measure. One confession demanded that we fulfill God's will "persistently and unswervingly. For you know well what is the reward of the servant who knowingly sins." If one intentional sin can damn us, then "everything which you have done unknowingly and now confess to have done wrongly, is forgiven you," but seemingly not known sins. Thus, the "gracious forgiveness of God and... the blood of Jesus Christ" can at times appear quite limited in Anabaptist thought (SA). While "all true believers are pleased to submit themselves in obedience to all commands of God" (33A), few if any Christians can say honestly that they have *never* resisted or disobeyed the will of God after being saved.

This overly exacting demand for perfection can be found in many corners of Anabaptism, leading its proponents to judge the salvation of fellow Anabaptists (not to mention those outside of the movement!) by a very rigid standard. This rigidity remains a hazard for modern Anabaptists, especially those who pride themselves on traditional expressions of Anabaptism that emphasize separation. To combat this danger, a strong emphasis on grace must remain in force even as we insist upon changed lives and obedience to Christ. If we are living out a pattern of seeking to follow and obey Christ out of love, there remains grace even when we fall short. A failure to acknowledge this leads us directly into the trap of a graceless gospel of works salvation which is no gospel at all. Anabaptists should look to confessions like this one, which argued of Christians that

> they must not believe in any way to be earning salvation by their works (Eph. 2:8; 2 Tim. 1:9), or that God is somehow still in debt to them for these things. But all believers must regard themselves as not other than as unnecessary servants (Luke 17:10), who are able to do nothing good through their own strength (John 15:6; 2 Cor. 3:5, 6). From the beginning, middle and end, it is only God the Lord who works the good in them through his own Spirit (Phil. 2:13)" (33A).

Or, to put it more simply, "It is not that we of ourselves are so strong. We confidently believe that the power and strength we have found in God has overcome death, the world, sin, and the devil" (HCF).

Assurance

Since Anabaptism gives a more complex answer to the question of whether one is saved by faith as opposed to works, it must also struggle to give a thorough answer to the question of Christian assurance—whether one can be confident that they are saved.

One confession gave a weak answer at this point. While the Confession of Jan Cents acknowledges that we can only follow God's commandments "in human weakness" and that we must rely on "the comforting intercession of Christ," it also suggests that the person who does follow Jesus in weakness will feel "a certain witness of his conscience and have a joyful hope" only "at the departure from this earth" (CJC).

But if Christ saves us despite our weakness, why can we not have confidence now—while we trust in him, love our neighbors, and seek to obey his commandments—that we are one with him and are saved so long as this trust remains? This is one area in which the early Anabaptists, perhaps out of a desire to counter the extreme confidence of Luther in salvation by faith alone, often left something to be desired.

Harrowing of Hell

Differing positions of Christ's descent into hell have been offered throughout church history. Some, particularly those who hold to soul sleep, deny that "hell" in this context is a place or realm but merely a circumlocution which means "death." For them, the creed simply means that Christ died. Others, like the early Anabaptists, perceive Jesus as bringing Old Testament saints out of hell. Another view which has been given increasing consideration is that 1 Pet 3:19's reference to Jesus preaching to spirits in prison (from which the creed's descent into hell is likely derived) refers to a proclamation of defeat against spiritual beings called the Watchers who (according to a popular first century reading of Gen 6) left their heavenly station to have sex with human women, further corrupting humanity in the process. While this view is the strangest, it also carries the most weight when one considers the context of first century Christianity and its influences, such as 1 Enoch.

While arguments can be marshaled for all of these views and others besides, only one presents itself in the major Anabaptist confessions. Further discussion is warranted.

Saved From...

As the result of Adam's sin, humanity is

> deprived of the beautiful paradise (Gen. 3:23); they must cover their nakedness; the woman is [subject] to the man's authority (1 Tim. 2:12); and children are born in suffering and pain (Gen. 3:18); and finally, [they will experience] temporal death and return again to dust and earth (Gen. 3:19; Heb. 9:28.) (33A).

God's work of salvation is to "redeem and eternally save us from the captivity of sin (2 Tim. 2:26), hell (1 Cor. 15:55), the devil and death" (33A). Though we were alienated from God, he intervened to "save and free men and women from their sins, guilt, and unrighteousness and restore them again to God's favour" (DC). In the upcoming sections, we will unpack how the early Anabaptists understood their salvation from death, hell, sin, and the wrath of God.

Death

Western Christianity has tended to focus on eternal conscious torment in hell as the primary consequence for Adam's sin, but Anabaptists also took special notice of the biblical witness that death is a result of sin. The Waterlander Confession states that "through transgression Adam seriously impaired his life, bringing upon himself and his posterity temporal and eternal death" (WC). Thus, "they were all driven out of the glorious paradise and garden to experience temporal and eternal death (Rom. 5:18)" (33A).

However, Christ the "Lord and conqueror over death, one who could no longer be held by the grave" (SC) "has freed the entire human race from the power of original sin, which is death" (WC). "In this he became to all believers a comforting assurance of their redemption and final resurrection from the dead" (SC).

Peter Riedemann therefore concludes, "He is the Saviour who has robbed death of its power, torn its bond and snare asunder and set us, his people, free" (AIO 1.6) and "whoever would rise again to immortal life must here be born anew to eternal life through faith in the truth" (HCF). Thus we look forward to the day when we shall "know him who is eternal life and makes us live eternally" (HCF).

One might conclude from these statements that Anabaptists believed that only the saved will live forever and the damned will go out of existence. However, the early Anabaptist confessions consistently speak in favor of the view of hell as eternal conscious torment.

Hell

Early Anabaptist confessions affirm that "because of [our] own guilt and perversity... he has promised [us] eternal punishment"

(WC). The quality of this eternal punishment is described in terms of conscious experience, thus the damned

> shall go into eternal fire and damnation, where they shall feel the pain of fire, where there shall be weeping and gnashing of teeth, likewise remaining there through all eternity, even as the blessed shall enjoy their happiness and salvation (13A).

Through the atonement provided by Jesus, individuals have an opportunity to be released from this fate, but those who reject this offer, "because of their own guilt and perversity, because they have put themselves outside of the will of God, and because they persist, without conversion, in running to the abyss of hell, he has promised [them] eternal punishment" (WC). Hell is defined in the early confessions as "a fiery pool and utmost darkness (Rev. 21:8), [wherein] all unbelievers finally must suffer the burning hell and eternal damnation" (33A). Moreover,

> there they will lie, not on beds of down, but on biting maggots, and covered with gnawing worms (Isa. 14:11). They will be tortured with flames of fire where their worm does not die and their fire is not quenched. The suffering of their torment will rise like the smoke from a fiery furnace and will last for ever and ever" (CJC).

Sin (Harmartiology)

Though Anabaptists have a more optimistic view of the human will's infection by sin than the Lutherans and Reformed, they nevertheless affirm that Adam's sin led to a moral corruption of his progeny:

> All originate out of an identical, sinful seed (Ps. 51:7; Job 14:4), and for this reason everyone from their youth on are inclined toward sin and evil (Gen. 6:5 and 8:21). Therefore, everyone has been captured by the power and authority of Satan and [are subject to] temporal and eternal death (Col. 1:13) (33A).

Since, however, humans do still possess the divine image (though corrupted), they have the ability to choose or reject God. This means that God cannot be blamed for the fate of the lost, since "the perishing and destruction of the unbelieving and godless comes only through themselves" (33A).

Of course our will, even enabled by the Spirit of God, is insufficient to save us without the sacrifice of Christ. Believers,

> through the promise of the redeemer, Jesus Christ, are delivered, freed and made righteous again, without their own good works, out of the eternal death and damnation into which they have fallen and lay submerged through Adam (33A).

In Anabaptist thought, we are not merely saved from *the judgment* which comes through sin, but we are actually saved from the enslaving power of sin and are given the ability to resist it: "This new birth brings with it a transformation of the will, of carnal desires and lust, a sincere putting to death of all evil within, of the old nature with its desires and life of sin and rebellion" (SC). This ability flows from our union with Christ and the Holy Spirit living inside of us. Therefore Riedemann wrote that "nothing takes place save what God works in men, as Paul says, 'Not I, but the grace of God,' and again, 'Not I live now, but Christ lives in me'" (AIO 2.24).

He went on to write that

> this Spirit of Christ which is promised and given to all believers makes them free from the law or power of sin, and plants them into Christ, makes them of his mind, yea, of his character and nature, so that they become one plant and one organism together with him: he the root or stem, we the branches, as he himself says, 'I am the true vine, ye, however, are the branches.' Thus we are one substance, matter, essence, yea, one bread and body with him—he the head, but we all members one of the other (AIO 2.24).

Thus, Anabaptists not only had an optimistic view of human nature as it relates to sin but also an optimistic view of what God can accomplish in us:

> He works in us and has taken away those sins from which we could not otherwise ever be freed. We served them long, but now, even if they do still stir in our members, they cannot rule over us any longer (HCF).

The wrath of God

Some strains of contemporary Christianity are rather uncomfortable with the notion of the wrath of God, and particularly with the claim that Jesus died to save us from it. For many of these Christians, other models of the atonement take center stage, such as the ransom theory which treats Christ's sacrifice as a payment to Satan for our release from his power. However, the early Anabaptists did not shy away from wrath language, understanding Christ's atonement as *at least* a means of appeasing the wrath of God and reconciling us to him.

The Thirty-Three Articles speak of Adam and Eve falling "through sin into the wrath and disfavor of God, and on the same day became subject to temporal and eternal death... they and their descendants" (33A). The Thirteen Articles give this solution to the problem of God's wrath upon us:

> Through this blood and death [Christ] has become a sacrifice, ransom, and payment for the sins of the world, through his death thus winning reconciliation for the sins of the world before the Father (13A).

Marpeck likewise speaks of Christ's atonement as necessary to deal with not only our sin but also our guilt:

> He, without guilt and sin, was sacrificed in history for the guilt and sin of man in order to restore the fall of man from the original love and raise him up into the blissful, joyful, eternally enduring love out of grace and more grace (AIO 1.7).

Finally, Simons also wrote of the atonement in terms of the propitiation of God:

> For it is He who stands between His Father and His imperfect children, with His perfect righteousness, and with His innocent blood and death, and intercedes for all those who believe on Him and who strive by faith in the divine Word to turn from evil, follow that which is good, and who sincerely desire with Paul that they may attain the perfection which is in Christ (CDS).

While Anabaptist thought is known for its nonviolent ethic, and many contemporary Anabaptists have applied this ethic to the atonement, early Anabaptists made a distinction between the wrath of God and the wrath of man. They were content to accept that God could be wrathful against sin while asking Christians to practice peace in anticipation of God's future, perfect judgment.

Reflections

The Nature of Hell

With few exceptions (such as Hans Denck's apparent universalism), the early Anabaptists tended to take the traditional view of eternal conscious torment for granted, not giving it the scrutiny that they gave to other traditional views like infant baptism and Christians fighting in war. In the intervening centuries, and in particular the last few decades, orthodox Christians who hold to a high view of Scripture have questioned eternal conscious torment, arguing that conditional immortality and even universal restoration have both a pedigree in the early church and supporting arguments that seem to be rooted in Scripture.

Whether or not these views hold up to biblical investigation as well as the traditional perspective does is a question beyond the scope of this volume. Nevertheless, Anabaptists have and should be keen to apply their radical "back to the Bible" approach to this issue as well by making the nature of hell a conversation in our churches and seminaries.

Sin with a Capital S

Modern scholarship has highlighted a hitherto largely overlooked aspect of Paul's view of sin—the notion of sin as an enslaving force that begins to take on an almost personal quality. In his Epistle to the Romans, Paul describes humans prior to being placed in Christ as not having much of a choice but to obey Sin

> any more than slaves (in the ordinary, social sense of the term) did in the ancient world... Sin causes someone to do what they do not want to do. Sin, then, is evidently not to be identified with the human self who wills to do what is good (as stipulated and determined by the Law) but cannot achieve it.[2]

This notion pairs well with other Anabaptist emphases, such as the spiritual rebirth that transforms and frees our wills. Further reflection from the Anabaptist vantage point could add considerable insights to this conversation.

Saved For...

In popular Christianity, salvation is often thought of as the means by which we achieve heaven and avoid hell. While this concern certainly features in the early Anabaptist confessions, it hardly exhausts their thought on this matter. We are not just saved *from* something bad but *for* something very good—union with God, life together in Christian community, holy living, and the proclamation of the gospel. For Anabaptists, what we are saved *for* is part and parcel to the message of salvation.

Union with God

A number of Anabaptist leaders seemed preoccupied with the idea of union with God. Riedemann, for example, wrote of the faith by

---

2. Martinus C. de Boer, in Gupta and Goodrich, *Sin and Its Remedy in Paul*, loc. 492.

which men "might be planted and grafted into Christ" (AIO 2.25). The result of this grafting is that all the members of Christ will be

> of one mind and intention (so that they want only to be like Christ, to partake of his nature, and diligently to do his will), cleaving to him as a bride and spouse to her bridegroom, yea, as one body with him, one plant, one tree, bearing and giving one kind of fruit (AIO 5.9).

In contrast to the Reformers, far less attention was given by Anabaptists to the initial faith by which we are grafted into Christ than the importance of living out that grafting in our daily lives. Thus Riedemann describes what union with Christ actually looks like in practice:

> This Spirit of Christ which is promised and given to all believers makes them free from the law or power of sin, and plants them into Christ, makes them of his mind, yea, of his character and nature, so that they become one plant and one organism together with him: he the root or stem, we the branches, as he himself says, 'I am the true vine, ye, however, are the branches.' Thus we are one substance, matter, essence, yea, one bread and body with him—he the head, but we all members one of the other." (AIO 2.24)

Simons likewise describes what living out our union with God looks like: that each sincere Christian becomes

> so united and mingled with God that he becomes a partaker of the divine nature and is made conformable to the image of his Son, who is the first of the born again and of those who rose with him from the sleep and death of sin (AIO 7.11).

From a modern evangelical perspective, the Anabaptist emphasis on union with God and becoming partakers in God's divine nature may seem strange and even irreverent. However, it is rooted in Scripture (2 Pet 1:4, Gal 2:20) and has been affirmed from Christian groups like the Eastern Orthodox (particularly in their doctrine of theosis) to Reformation leaders such as John

Calvin (see Marcus Peter Johnson's *One With Christ: An Evangelical Theology of Salvation*). The retrieval of this doctrine would not only be a return to early Anabaptist teaching but to biblical and ecumenical Christian teaching.

Union with God means that our good works "are not man's works but God's, since the willing and the ability to turn to God are not of man but the gift of God through Jesus Christ our Lord" (AIO 2.15). This language of oneness with Christ is appropriate for Anabaptism since it focuses much more on salvation in its totality as opposed to an individual choice made in a moment of time to believe. To be saved is to be in Christ, because "no living man who is outside Jesus Christ can be justified before God" (PM, V, 2).

Life Together (Ecclesiology)

Early Anabaptists placed a great deal of emphasis on their doctrine of the church. Instead of the church being a diversion for Christians while waiting for Jesus to come back, or a support group for keeping us focused on Jesus, one might even say that from an Anabaptist perspective, life together is what we are saved *for*.

While the Protestants' belief in state Christianity led them to make a strong distinction between the visible (state) and invisible (saved) church, the early Anabaptists would have none of it—there is only one church and it

> consists of all people upon the face of the earth who, through the power of God, have come to a renewal of their inner being by grace, in whom the true likeness and mind of Christ dwells, and who are truly obedient to God (WC).

From a church leadership structure perspective, Anabaptism has been marked by a spirit of unanimity and consent in its local congregations, which some might argue makes a clergy/laity distinction unnecessary. However, early Anabaptist confessions nevertheless consistently taught that offices of leadership were important to the church's proper function. Indeed, "the church can neither exist and grow nor continue as a structure without offices and ordination" (DC). One of these offices is that of deacon, which functioned for Anabaptists in much the same way that it did in the early chapters of the book of Acts. The purpose of this office was to "look after and minister to the poor... [Deacons] receive gifts and alms and in turn faithfully distribute them, with all honesty as is becoming, to the saints in need" (DC). In addition, elders teach the word, administer sacraments, and give guidance to the church. Various Anabaptist communities and traditions had additional offices and different types of organizational structures, but the sense that leadership is necessary has been a consistent refrain.

Often, the spirit of unanimity and the felt need for leadership came together in a complementary fashion. According to the Prussian Confession, ministers were often chosen by God through the unanimous consent of the congregation:

> Now when the church requires such persons to be servants of the Word, they together pray earnestly to God... that he, who knows every heart, will show through a united voice, whom he has chosen for such a service and office (PC).

Speaking of the church more generally, Menno Simons wrote that the true signs of the church are "an unadulterated, pure doctrine," "a scriptural use of the sacramental signs," "obedience to the Word," "unfeigned, brotherly love," "a bold confession of God and Christ" and "oppression and tribulation for the sake of the Lord's Word" (AIO 5.11). We will discuss these marks and others in the following sub-sections.

Unity

The church of God is joined together "as members of one body... through the faith and bonds of love, being united to each other according to Christ Jesus." Among early Anabaptists, unity and intimacy was expected to mark each community in Christ as believers lived "according to the one rule of the divine word (Phil. 3:16), and with mutual love are bound together to each other (Phil. 2:2), and thus have fellowship with each other" (33A).

Dirk Philips highlighted the necessity of the head (Jesus) being connected to the body (church) in order for its members to live and thrive together, and how the sacrament of the Lord's Supper reminds us of this reality each time we partake of it:

> For in the body of Christ two things are especially noted, namely, the Head and the members. The Head, which is Christ, reminds us that from it we all receive grace and life (Eph. 1:23), and that one must cleave to the Head alone... With the gifts which we receive from God—be they spiritual or natural—we likewise serve our members for the perfecting and edifying of the body of Christ, and all this in love (AIO 6.15).

Stewardship

Church historian Walter Klaassen describes the Anabaptist movement as one in which "property could be held privately, but [it] could never be absolutely private. Property was viewed as a trust from God" (AIO 11). Hubmaier certainly lends support to this reading with this statement about the community of goods:

> Each man should have regard for his neighbor, so that the hungry might be fed, the thirsty refreshed, the naked clothed. For we are not lords of our own property, but stewards and dispensers. Assuredly no one could say that we claim that one should take his own from anybody and make it common property; rather we would say: if anyone would take your cloak, give him your coat also (AIO 11.1).

While sharing was not something to be mandated by force, Anabaptists differed on whether followers of Christ were expected to have all things in common or simply to be generous with what God had entrusted to them. Thus, a confession from the Swiss Brethren affirms that "children of God may purchase their own properties, own them and use them if the opportunity presents itself" (CH), but the Hutterite theologian Ulrich Stadler argued that the language of "'one, common' builds the Lord's house and is pure." In contrast, the one who says of physical objects, "'mine, thine, his, own' divides the Lord's house and is impure." More than that, he may even be "outside of Christ and his communion and has thus no Father in heaven" (AIO 5.6).

The Hutterite theologian Peter Riedemann was perhaps the greatest explainer of his movement's philosophy about communal property, a philosophy which was largely derived from passages in the first few chapters of the book of Acts. He wrote:

> All of God's gifts, not only the spiritual but also the temporal, have been given so that they not be kept but be shared with each other... Paul says one person should not have an abundance while another suffers want; instead, there should be equality... The more a person is attached to property and claims ownership of things, the further away he is from the fellowship of Christ and from being in the image of God (HCF).

However, even Riedemann had to acknowledge that the practice of communal ownership is not attested to in all of the faithful communities in the New Testament:

> Someone may say that this only applies to what took place in Jerusalem and therefore does not apply today. In reply, we say that even if it did only happen in Jerusalem, it does not follow that it should not happen now. The apostles and the churches were not at fault, but the opportunity, the right means, and the right time were lacking (HCF).

While the Hutterites practice a much more collectivistic and communal form of Christianity, and this makes them somewhat distinct, the whole of early Anabaptists agreed that

> [Christians should serve one another] with temporal gifts for the body so that there will be no lack of physical necessities among any of the same members of the body (Acts 4:34), and that under this true Israel of God there will be no beggars (Deut. 15:4). They must, according to

their ability, show common love toward all people (2 Pet. 1:7; Gal. 6:12), even toward their enemies who persecute and kill them (Matt. 5:44) (33A).

Early Anabaptists also spoke out against avarice, which they defined as collecting "money and goods unjustly" (33A). Thus, not only certain attitudes toward money, but also occupations like moneylending were seen as inappropriate for Christians.

Simplicity

Simplicity may not be a new value for Anabaptists, but it is a noticeable distinctive in our prosperous modern era when Amish, conservative Mennonites, and Hutterites dress plainly, are suspicious of new technology, and work for necessities rather than extravagances.

Among the early Anabaptists, it was confessed that "all the arrogance, pride and pomp of this world [in words, works, dress, and manners] are an abomination and hated by God" (CH). They spoke against pride, which "reveals itself in clothing (Sir. 19:25; 1 Pet. 3:3; 1 Tim. 2:9), housing, speaking, eating, and drinking." Their proposed remedy for these carnal temptations was to "lay aside everything and arm yourselves against these with the humility of Christ" (33A).

Menno Simons gave another, more moderate suggestion—a detached attitude toward earthly things:

> Their citizenship is in heaven, and they use the lower creations such as eating, drinking, clothing, and shelter, with thanksgiving and to the necessary support of their own lives, and to the free service of their neighbor, according to the Word of the Lord (AIO 5.7).

Early Anabaptists were also suspicious of merchant occupations because of their associations with "temporal greed and the vanity of ostentatious clothing, which imitate the world rather than displaying the humility of Christ" (CC). Some communities treated such occupations as verboten for brothers in the fellowship, while others urged a cautious approach to working in that field which was informed by the values of simplicity and humility. In short, Anabaptists sought to work for the necessities of life and eschewed what they saw as frivolities so that they might focus on Christ and share any excess they had with brothers and sisters in the Lord.

Separation

While 16th- and 17th-century Roman Catholics and Protestants believed in a Christianity which was tightly integrated with the affairs of the world, Anabaptists took seriously the idea that Christians are supposed to live apart from the world—that we're called to be different. At Schleitheim, some of the earliest Anabaptists described themselves as those "who have been and shall be separated from the world in all that we do and leave undone" (SA). Their doctrine of separation tended toward dualism. They argued that

> there is nothing else in the world and all creation than good or evil, believing and unbelieving, darkness and light, the world and those who are [come] out of the world, God's temple and idols, Christ and Belial, and none will have part with the other. [God] admonishes us therefore to go out from Babylon and from the earthly Egypt, that we may not be partakers in their torment and suffering, which the Lord will bring upon them (SA).

Instead of seeing the Europe of its day as a Christian continent, Anabaptists saw Europe as Babylon and true Christians as a separated remnant. They were those who "turn their ears to the voice of God that calls (Matt. 11:28; Isa. 1:10), and who have separated themselves from the world with all its sinful lusts" (33A).

As a rule, the theology of separation beat out concerns for ecumenism and charity toward Catholics and Protestants. Riedemann wrote that "all baptizers of children have forsaken the church and community of Christ and separated themselves from the same" (AIO 16.6). A tract sometimes attributed to Sattler cautioned against listening to "the papist or Lutheran preachings" on the basis that we are called to "flee from such desolation and abomination and in no way turn back to it." Those moderates who claimed that "infant baptism is indifferent and one can baptize infants without detriment to the truth" were certainly "in league with the Lutherans, hoping perhaps henceforth to be able to live without the cross" (LMS 9). The Schleitheim Articles, generally understood to have been from the hand of Sattler, stated that "everything which has not been united with our God in Christ is nothing but an abomination which we should shun. By this are meant all popish and repopish [meaning Protestant] works and idolatry" (SA).

There were some exceptions to this rule, however. Pilgram Marpeck could at times approach his theological differs with a degree of charity and hope for reconciliation, as he did in some of his disputations with the Protestant reformer Martin Bucer. In return, Bucer referred to Marpeck as a "stiff-necked heretic" whose "nice unblameable conduct" made his heresy all the more dangerous for its attractiveness (PM, Introduction).

Communal Discipline

Walter Klaassen noted that amongst the early Anabaptists, community discipline was treated as the Anabaptist alternative to state violence. Where the world takes up the sword to keep its members in line, the church uses the nonviolent "ban" in love to pressure fellow brothers and sisters into giving up sin. Thus,

> nonresistance is not simply a matter of refusing to bear arms in wartime, although that is certainly included. Rather it is a totally new life orientation in which all human relationships are governed by patience, understanding, love, forgiveness, and a desire for the redemption even of the enemy (AIO 13.0).

The Schleitheim Articles provide a perfect example of this dichotomy:

> Now Christ says to the woman who was taken in adultery, not that she should be stoned according to the law of His Father (and yet He says, 'what the Father commanded me, that I do') but with mercy and forgiveness and the warning to sin no more, says: 'Go, sin no more.' Exactly thus should we also proceed, according to the rule of the ban (SA).

In the "ban," the believing community shunned or excluded an errant brother or sister in order to persuade them to change their behavior. The confessions consistently teach that this must be done in love to keep their brothers on the straight and narrow path following Jesus. As Sattler said elsewhere, "Christians admonish benevolently, out of sympathy and compassion for the sinful, and do not legalistically coerce persons this way or that" (LMS 1). The Waterlander Confession spells this out clearly, arguing that the ban was used

> in order that [a sinning brother] may be restored and won again, that his soul may be won, and that those who hear and institute the admonition may in brotherly love, forget and cover his transgression. On the other hand, we confess that the stubborn and deliberate sinner or transgressor, after sufficient admonition by the congregation shall be separated and cut off from the body of Christ to God's honor; that his church may remain pure and an instrument for the conversion of the fallen (WC).

This confession, which presented a milder approach to church discipline than was practiced by some Anabaptists, acknowledged that

> [one should] neither eat nor drink with [a banned brother] that they may be shamed and corrected. Nevertheless, since the ban should lead to healing, we do not wish to be so hard that fellowship should be denied him in time of need (WC).

The Anabaptists who wrote the Dordrecht Confession concurred, arguing that shunning ought to be used in Christian moderation so that it may have the effect not of destroying but of healing the sinner... If he is in need, hungry, thirsty, naked, ill, or in any form of want, then we ought—according to the love and teaching of Christ and his apostles—to help and give him assistance. Otherwise, the shunning leads to ruin instead of correction or amendment (DC).

Pilgram Marpeck disputed with the Swiss Brethren over their use of the ban, which he argued they applied with too great frequency and too little compassion. He reminded them that Jesus encouraged his hearers to discern whether a person is in sin by their fruits: "He does not say by the blossoms or the foliage" (PM, V, 2). In other words, what might look suspicious to a weak brother may not really be sin at all: David's wife Michal shamed David when he danced for joy at the coming of the ark of the covenant into Jerusalem, Jesus was judged by the Jewish leaders for eating with sinners and healing on the sabbath, and some Anabaptists were quick to judge others as outside of the body of Christ for infractions of community rules which Marpeck said did not derive from God:

> Whoever murders, wounds, and burdens an innocent conscience with his own commands and prohibitions, outside of God's commandment and prohibition, robs God of His honor, murders souls, and tramples the Son of God with his feet. He derides and makes a mockery of the sacrifice of Jesus Christ, with which he is bought (PM, V, 2).

Marpeck feared that when discipline was practiced too harshly, one risked cutting off a member of the body prematurely—an action which would compromise health and wholeness if applied to a human body, which Paul compared the church to. Thus, he urged not judging by appearances which can be deceiving. After all, "there are many blossoms and appearances of good which conceal the most gruesome reality, as in Papists, Lutherans, Zwinglians, and false Anabaptists." Instead, Marpeck wrote that we should warn a brother out of loving concern when the "leaves" or "blossoms" looked suspicious but avoid using the ban until the fruit could be clearly discerned (PM, V, 2).

Despite disagreement on application, early Anabaptists agreed that the practice of the ban, "which was established to shame and convert sinners" would "keep the church pure" (CJC). Consistent with the Anabaptist belief that the visible church *was* the real church, church discipline allowed the fellowship to "be kept pure and free of scandals so that the name of the Lord be not dishonoured and the church be not an offense to those who are without" (DC).

Sacraments

Sacraments are ordinances that the church is called to observe, and through which God imparts grace to the fellowship of believers.

Early Anabaptist confessions acknowledge two sacraments, baptism and the Lord's Supper. They were described as "external, visible actions and undeserved divine grace." "In these holy sacraments alone is appropriated the fruit, power, and worth of his work upon the cross" (SC).

On the other hand,

> neither baptism, nor the Lord's Supper, nor church membership, nor any other outward ceremony can without faith, the new birth, and the amendment of life make it possible for us to please God and to receive the solace and promise of salvation (DC).

Thus, in these sacraments God is doing something for the church and its members—they are not mere reminders. However, they are, on their own, simply external actions which can accomplish nothing if not paired with an inward reality. In modern parlance, one might say that they are vehicles of grace, but they can get us nowhere without the fuel of our sincere faith.

Although marriage is not traditionally seen as a sacrament in Anabaptist and Protestant thought, the institution of Christian marriage is given so much attention in the early confessions that it seemed appropriate to include it here.

Baptism

Anabaptists only baptized those who were old enough to plausibly confess sincere belief and a commitment to Christ. This distinction set them apart from their Roman Catholic and Protestant contemporaries, both of whom practiced infant baptism for both theological and political reasons. A baptized baby was thought to be a member not merely of the church but also of the Christian nation. Church historian Walter Klaassen noted that both Catholics and Protestants held to the concept of the *Volkskirche* or state-church. With

> the exception of heretics and Jews everyone in Europe belonged to it by virtue of [infant] baptism... each country had an official faith of which all citizens were assumed to be adherents. [But for Anabaptism, the church was] the gathered congregation of believers who have voluntarily entered it by baptism upon confession of faith (AIO 5).

In short, the Anabaptist insistence upon sincere repentance as a prerequisite to being part of Christ's body made infant baptism a contradiction in terms. Anabaptists denied that the apostolic church ever practiced infant baptism, and that they were thus "united and at one with Christ and his holy apostles in [their] practice of baptising believers" (KC). Believers' baptism was a crystallization of their belief that the only real Christian is a fully committed one who chooses to come and die in order to follow Jesus for his own sake.

Early Anabaptist confessions spoke of Christian baptism as being performed both internally and externally—"internally with the Holy Spirit and fire, outwardly with water, in the name of the Father, the Son and the Holy Spirit" (CH). The external, visible baptism testifies and signifies that Jesus Christ himself baptizes the repentant believer inwardly with the bath of the new birth and renewal through the Holy Spirit, washing the soul from all filth and sin through the merit of his shed blood (SC).

However, "external baptism with water does not really [bring the one who is baptized] into the kingdom of God... It is merely a sign and proof of the grace and blood of Christ, the washing away of sins." If there is no internal baptism with the Holy Spirit, "the visible baptism of the water (like the seal of an empty letter) (Rom. 2:8) is vain and useless" (33A).

Through this twofold baptism, "believers are joined together through one Spirit with Christ (1 Cor. 12:13) in the fellowship" and "also rise up with Christ in a new life, walking according to the Spirit" (33A).

Marpeck situated Paul's view of baptism as a kind of death within the context of biblical theology, noting that

> wherever water is mentioned in the Scriptures, it refers to tribulation, anxiety, distress, and suffering, and the depth of water is spoken of as physical death. That is the sign of Jonah, in which the whole world is corrupted and condemned to death (PM, III).

Thus, the imagery of water found in Noah's flood, in the crossing of the Red Sea, and in Jonah's return (as it seemed) from the dead made water baptism a perfect picture of the death of the old man and resurrection to new spiritual life. This made it the ideal sign for formal entry into the Christian life.

Some Anabaptists spoke of a

> threefold baptism, the inner baptism of the Spirit, water baptism, and the baptism of blood. The baptism of blood was the experience of tribulation and suffering. For Hubmaier and most Anabaptists this meant persecution. For [Hans] Hut, however, it meant also, and more importantly, the experience of desolation and tribulation that each person encounters as he is liberated from dependence on all external things (AIO 8).

Indeed, Hubmaier wrote, "I confess three types of baptism: that of the Spirit given internally in faith; that of water given externally through the oral confession of faith before the church; and that of blood in martyrdom or on the deathbed. Christ spoke of the latter in Luke 12" (AIO 8.4).

The question of whether suffering is required to be a faithful Christian is one we will return to in our reflections.

The Lord's Supper

Roman Catholic theology holds that the bread and wine of communion are transubstantiated into the body and blood of Jesus. The Protestant reformers debated how and to what extent the elements truly did become the body and blood of Christ, with Zwingli taking on the furthest opposition to transubstantiation with his symbolic view.

Anabaptists, as was their custom, questioned the very validity of the question. As Klaassen notes, "They regarded such a discussion as totally beside the point." The real issue that the Lord's Supper points to is not the presence of Christ in a loaf of bread but the presence of Christ in believers. Klaassen continues:

> All strands of Anabaptism give evidence of a twofold interpretation of the Supper. It was, on the one hand, a remembrance of the love of Christ which expressed itself in dying for his own. Jesus and his sacrifice were the foundation of Christian life and of the church. On the other hand, the Supper was seen as a celebration of the oneness and unity of the church brought about by Christ's death (AIO 9.0).

The confessions bear this out. "Just as the bread and wine are received with the mouth," the Confession of Hesse states, "so also the heavenly body, the flesh and blood of Jesus Christ, are received by the believing soul spiritually in faith" (CH). The unity of the church is "represented and signified in the breaking of the bread" (DC). For those who take it in the right spirit, the Supper "unites us in peace, love, oneness of spirit, and true Christian communion among ourselves" (PC).

Anabaptist leaders developed these ideas in rich ways. Simons wrote that, in addition to its pointing to the remission of sins through "the innocent flesh and blood of our Lord Jesus Christ alone," the Lord's Supper is "proof and testimony that [we] are one in Christ and his holy church" (AIO 2.27). Thus,

> it is an emblem of Christian love, of unity, and of peace in the church of Christ. Paul says, For we, being many, are one bread and one body; for we are all partakers of that one bread. 1 Cor. 10:17. For as a loaf being composed of many grains is but one bread; so we also being composed of many members are but one body in Christ. And as the members of a natural body are not disharmonious, but are altogether united and at one among themselves; so it is with all those who are in Spirit and faith true members of the body of Christ. For this reason this same supper was called by Tertullian a brotherly meal or love feast (AIO 9.15).

Conrad Grebel wrote that bread is "the outer bond," but love "is the inner bond," and that "the Supper is an expression of fellowship, not a Mass and sacrament. Therefore none is to receive it alone, neither on his deathbed nor otherwise... It should be used much and often" (AIO 9.1).

Riedemann waxes poetic in his description of the Lord's Supper:

> In taking the bread and giving it to his disciples, Christ desires to show and explain the community of his body to his disciples, that they had become one body, one plant, one living organism and one nature with him.

Thus the Lord's Supper points to a deeper reality, that each Christian "is grafted into and becomes a fellow-member of his nature and character, whereby we are also all led into the one mind and will of Christ" (AIO 9.13). Because it points to our union with Christ, it should be observed by Jesus' "holy and dear disciples alone, who have been born of the Holy Spirit, have forsaken all, and have followed after him the way of the cross in all oppression, scorn and suffering" (KC).

The early Anabaptists therefore treated the sacrament with solemnity for the grace which it carries, but also with practicality since "hearts can never be cleansed from sin [solely] through bread and wine" (KC).

Marriage

Similar to Protestants and Catholics, the early Anabaptists held

> marriage to be an ordinance of God, as was the first marriage (Gen. 2:22; Matt. 19:9), instituted in such a manner that every husband shall have his own and only wife, and every wife her own and only husband (1 Cor. 7:2; Eph. 5:31) (SC).

Riedemann argued that this union was not strictly egalitarian but that it was the third level of a series of relationships wherein one part of a union must obey the other:

> Marriage consists of three stages or levels. First is the union of God with the soul or spirit, then that of the spirit with the body, and third that of one person with another, that is, a man with a woman. This is not the first but the last and lowest level... As the man is head of the woman, so the spirit is head of the body, and God is head of the spirit (HCF).

Though some stricter Anabaptist fellowships held to a form of the ban which dictated that an "erring spouse, whether husband or wife, must be avoided and shunned" (WA), other groups argued that a married couple cannot be separated even by "ban, belief or unbelief, anger, quarrels or hardness of heart," though "with the exception of adultery" (CH) or "death" (33A). In the case of a "deliberate adulterer... the innocent party is free [to remarry], provided that she confers with the congregation and remarries, according to opportunity, and concludes the matter with understanding" (WA).

Anabaptists also followed Paul's additional guidance to married couples in 1 Corinthians:

> If [an] unbeliever desires to separate from his spouse for reasons of faith, then the believer shall conduct herself honestly without marrying [another] for as long as the unbeliever is not remarried. But if the unbeliever marries, or commits adultery, then the believer may also marry, in accordance with the counsel of the elders and the congregation (WA).

In addition, Anabaptists heeded the advice of Paul that marriage was not necessarily an expectation for Christian believers or something that every Christian should seek to attain:

> Anyone who has no need for [marriage], and who can maintain himself pure and undefiled in a state of virginity in order to serve the Lord better and without hindrance (1 Cor. 7:35), is even more highly praised. Therefore the estate of marriage is a free concession for each one, and not a command (1 Cor. 7:6) (33A).

Just as singleness was a way of life that was available to one who preferred it, marriage was likewise treated as a voluntary compact between a consenting man and a consenting woman: "In the church of God a brother may take as his wife a sister in the faith (2 Cor. 6:15; Deut. 7:3) and the sister has the freedom to accept or reject his [offer]" (PC).

Holy Living

While it would be false to say that Protestants didn't care about sanctification or obedience, in their division of justification and sanctification, justification took center stage. The Anabaptists, on the other hand, saw initial justification as merely the entree to union with Christ and his body, the church. Thus, even believers' baptism, which was seen as a distinguishing mark of the movement, was primarily the means of incorporating "all believers into the body of Christ, of which He is the head... As the head is minded, so must its members also be" (LMS 1).

Since God has made us "partakers of his divine nature" (SC), Christians are those who "are new born spiritual persons... and known by their fruits" (KC). Becoming a new creature means that "the old life of sin has passed away and everything has been made new" (KC). This new birth which God effects causes

> a restoring of the image of God in us, a renewing of mind and heart... a transformation of the will, of carnal desires and lust, a sincere putting to death of all evil within, of the old nature with its desires and life of sin and rebellion (SC).

Christ's church "is known by her character" (33A), which is to say that those who are born again "live in love (which the Holy Spirit has poured into their hearts)" (SC). In

> putting on the true character of the love of Christ... [we] learn from him how to be humble and meek of heart (Matt. 11:29) since he, as a humble lamb, did not open his mouth (to vengeance against his persecutors and killers) (Isa. 53:10; 1 Pet. 2:25) but prayed for the same out of love (Luke 23:33) (33A).

It is love that is "the principal garb and characteristic of the true followers of Christ," "the sum of the great commandments," and "the fulfillment of the law." "It binds believers in a harmonious relationship with the Lord [and] as one heart and soul to each other in peace and unity." Love for the brethren means forgiving each other and dealing gently with each other. It means not increasing the hurt of the injured nor oppressing or rejecting the weak. "Instead each esteems the other person more than himself" (DC).

Christians "will necessarily... produce and show from their faith good works and virtues" (33A). Thus it is not sufficient just to believe the right things, since true "believers must live according to the word of the Lord and the blameless example of Christ and his apostles" (33A). These good works do not originate from us "but the grace from God which man encounters is a complete rebirth from flesh, sin, death, and hell to grace in the peace, joy, and comfort of the Holy Spirit" (PM, V, 2).

Hutter, echoing the apostle Paul, wrote that "all those who live and walk in the spirit do not fulfill the lusts of the flesh" (AIO 2.20). Riedemann spoke of the renewing power of faith which "makes him like God in nature" (AIO 2.24).

The obedience which flows from this new nature is not the obedience of a slave but of a son: "The servile [obedience] springs out of love of reward or of self. The filial ever does as much as it can, apart from any command" (LMS 8). If we are adopted as God's sons and share in his nature by grace, then this will necessarily result in a change of behavior.

The Holy Spirit of course plays an essential function in our growth in holiness by

> eradicating and destroying the sin that we have by nature so that what is good, true, and holy, which he brings with him and plants in us, may take root and bear fruit" (HCF).

Since Anabaptists affirmed many of the high ethical views of Catholics and Protestants of their day, we will look at three areas where they differed.

Nonviolence and Non-Participation in the State

One of the most important and well-known distinctives of Anabaptists are their views on nonviolence and non-participation in the state.

Anabaptists, largely though not exclusively on the basis of Rom 13, held that "God, who is king of all kings and lord of all lords... has established kings and government in all lands" (PC) and "instituted civil government for the punishment of evil and the protection of the good as well as to govern the world and to provide good regulations and policies in cities and countries" (DC). Governance is necessary because without it "the world (being over run with evil) (1 John 5:19) cannot survive" (33A). Since "there is no government without it being of God" (PC), "we may not resist, despise, or condemn the state. We should recognize it as a minister of God" (DC). Indeed, "we should constantly and earnestly pray for the state and the welfare of the country that under its protection we may lead a quiet and peaceful life in all godliness and honesty" (DC). While governments should be challenged when they overextend their God-ordained function, Anabaptists "in no way seek to despise or judge honest government nor give it a lesser place than that given by the Holy Spirit through the writings of the Apostle Paul" (SC).

Despite these pious words about government when properly administered, God's purpose for human government is often expressed in negative terms. Riedemann, for instance, wrote that "governmental authority was not given from grace but from disfavor and anger, because the people had turned away from God" and thus "the government is a picture for us, a sign and reminder of people's estrangement from God." In other words,

> God has established government because people turned away from him and lived according to their own desires... That is why after the Flood he established the government to be a rod of his anger, to shed the blood of those who have shed blood (HCF).

Marpeck concurred. He wrote that

> the wisdom of the office of the worldly rulers is designed to work through the external sword in vindictiveness, mercilessness, hate of sin, physical vengeance, killing of evildoers, worldly natural governments, judgments, and similar things (AIO 12.16).

Anabaptists taught that a rightly ordered government will not harass the people of God but will limit its function to do "nothing else except advance justice, protect the righteous and punish the evil doer" (CH), namely criminals like "murderers, robbers, [and] arsonists" (KC). Riedemann argued that the authorities were ordained by God to avenge against "those who have shed blood"

(HCF), thus seemingly limiting the function of government to protecting and avenging the innocent against the violent. However, Simons argued that the state should also threaten "sodomites, adulterers, seducers, sorcerers" and "deceivers" of the religious variety, making the line between church and state more permeable than many Anabaptists would find appropriate (AIO 15.8).

Although Anabaptists often spoke of the state in idealistic language, they also acknowledged that it regularly failed to serve its divinely ordained purpose. Oftentimes, instead of serving God, those in power "are persecutors of Christians and enemies of the cross; for rubbish is their god and condemnation is their end" (KC). Simons railed against the state's selfish and corrupt warmaking, writing that

> Captains, knights, foot soldiers, and similar bloody men risk body and soul for the sake of gain, and swear with uplifted fingers that they are ready to destroy cities and countries, to take citizens and inhabitants, to kill them and take their possessions, although these have never harmed them nor given them so much as an evil word. O God, what cursed, wicked abomination and traffic! And they call that protecting the country and the people, and assisting in justice (AIO 11.9)!

Hubmaier warned "all those whom God has girded with the sword, not to use it against innocent blood with persecution, imprisonment, hanging, drowning, or burning" because "the shed and martyred blood will cry out against them to heaven." Despite their status as ministers of God, Hubmaier contended that "it will not help you to say: I was forced to do so; my master bade me do it; he would have it thus. Nay, not so. One must obey God rather than man" (AIO 12.1). Hubmaier had the distinction of being the only mainstream Anabaptist leader who approved of a church-state relationship and even war, but unlike some of the Protestants and Catholics of his day, he only approved of defensive war—not holy war and certainly not war for profit.

Perhaps because he didn't have to make allowances for church and state intermingling, as Hubmaier did, Jakob Hutter's language on this subject was more strident:

> Woe, we say to you! who fear more that frail and mortal man than the living, omnipotent and eternal God, and chase from you, suddenly and inhumanely, the children of God, the afflicted widow, the desolate orphan, and scatter them abroad... Great slaughter, much misery and anguish, sorrow, and adversity, yea, everlasting groaning, pain and torment, are daily appointed you. The Most High will lift his hand against you, now and eternally (AIO 12.11).

Nevertheless, even when governance was in the wrong,

> no one should rise up or oppose with one's own power or with outward weapons, nor fight against the authorities in this way. Such a person will fall to the wrath and punishment of God, and also to the punishment of the authorities (KC).

Instead of taking up the sword against their oppressors, Anabaptists would rather "flee from one city or country to another" and "suffer the loss of goods rather than bring harm to another." Modeling their behavior after the Sermon on the Mount, Anabaptists would "pray for our enemies and, if they are hungry or thirsty, feed and refresh them and thus assure them of our good will and desire to overcome evil with good" (DC).

This summarizes the Anabaptist view of the state. Next we will turn to why they thought Christians could not participate in it, or at least in its violent functions.

First of all, the kingdom of God which all sincere Christians are part of is distinct from and excludes the kingdoms of men. In Christ, Christians "come into our kingdom, fatherland, and citizenship." This citizenship "is in heaven and not on earth. Christians are the members of the household of God and fellow citizens of the saints, and not of the world." Since it is heavenly and spiritual, "flesh and blood, pomp and temporal, earthly honor and the world cannot comprehend the kingdom of Christ. In sum: There is nothing in common between Christ and Belial" (LMS 1).

The Thirty-Three Articles add that

> since Christ's kingdom is spiritual and not of this world (John 18:36), so he has also dissuaded and forbidden all of his ministers and disciples from all worldly ruling and highness (Matt. 20:26; Mark 10:43; Luke 22:26) allowing the worldly office to be a part of the worldly regiment (33A).

Since the citizenship of secular governments is in the world, but that of "the Christians is in heaven," likewise the weapons of governments "are carnal and only against the flesh, but the weapons of Christians are spiritual, against the fortification of the devil" (SA).

Sincere followers of Christ who know his word will understand that "no other outward weapon is given or commanded except alone this spiritual sword, which is the word of God." Therefore we "do not desire to protect ourselves with weapons of outer steel" (KC). "The diabolical weapons of violence such as sword, armor, and the like" shall "fall away from" those who obey Christ's words: "you shall not resist evil" (SA). Believing Isaiah's prophecy about the Messiah has already come to pass, true Christians "have changed their carnal weapons, their swords, into ploughshares and their spears into sickles. They neither lift a sword, nor teach, nor participate in carnal warfare" (SC).

While violence and domination are inextricably tied to the princes of this world, "the violence of the sword" has been forbidden to us by Christ (SA). All the things which worldly power does, "the waging of war, the destroying of life and property of the enemy... do not harmonize with the new life in Christ." Thus, "He has also not called his disciples or followers to be worldly kings, princes, dukes, or authorities, nor instructed them to seek and assume such office, nor to rule the world in a worldly manner" (SC).

Since "it is not proper for a Christian to be a magistrate" (AIO 12.12), it is likewise not proper for a magistrate who accepts Jesus to remain in his position. Riedemann mused:

> If rulers divest themselves of their glory as Christ did, and humble themselves with him and allow Christ, only, to use them, then the way to life would be as open to them as to others. But when Christ begins to work in men, he does nothing except what he himself did—and he fled when men sought to make him a king (AIO 12.15).

Pilgram Marpeck, as was his custom, took a moderate but principled stance to Christians in government. He made room for Christians to serve in some civil roles, but contended that

> no true Christian may administer cities and protect countries, nor people as an earthly lord. Nor may he use force, for that is the function of earthly and temporal rulers but never of true Christians (AIO 12.16).

Because Christian faith to an Anabaptist was always entered into volitionally and with abandon, it is understandable that they would distinguish strongly between the world (even a nominally Christian world) and the church.

The Anabaptist historian Watler Klaassen notes:

> In a society in which everyone was regarded as Christian there was no longer a world into which the offending member could be excommunicated. The only way of getting rid of an incorrigible heretic was to put him to death... Anabaptists saw a clear distinction between church and world. When, therefore, someone was excommunicated, that person was sent out of the church, God's kingdom, into the world, the kingdom of Satan (AIO 10).

In this way, Anabaptism's belief in the notion of Christianity as a separated remnant helped insulate them from being persuaded to accept the culture of religious violence which pervaded their time and place. For them,

> the sword is an ordering of God outside the perfection of Christ... But within the perfection of Christ only the ban is used for the admonition and exclusion of the one who has sinned, without the death of the flesh, simply the warning and the command to sin no more (SA).

To those Christians who felt that it was appropriate to take up *both* sword *and* cross, Menno Simons chastised, borrowing language from Paul:

> O foolish Galatians, who hath bewitched you, that ye should not obey the truth, before whose eyes Christ Jesus hath been evidently set forth, crucified among you? This only would I learn of you, whether you are baptized on the sword or on the cross? So foolish are ye, having begun in the Spirit are ye now made perfect by the flesh? Have ye suffered so many things in vain, if it be yet in vain? (BJL).

The early Anabaptists largely ignored scriptural data regarding the demonic influence over political power which would have both supported and nuanced their position. Instead, they argued that there are two kingdoms, both of which serve the purposes of God—a spiritual one which serves spiritual goods and a temporal one which serves temporal ones.

However, at times they did seem to suggest that the kingdoms of men which oppressed them were serving another power besides God. For instance, the *Short Confession of Faith and the Essential Elements of Christian Doctrine* notes a partnership between "the spirits of evil under heaven with their associates upon earth" (SC). Michael Sattler also suggests a link more than once. In the *Schleitheim Articles* he writes of "the diabolical weapons of violence" and in a chain of argumentation elsewhere, he reasons that Christ "has no kingdom in the world, but that which is of this world is against His kingdom." Moreover, "the devil is prince over the whole world, in whom all the children of darkness rule." Since therefore, the citizenship of Christians is in heaven and not on earth... earthly honor cannot comprehend the kingdom of Christ." In short, "there is nothing in common between Christ and Belial" (LMS 1).

More discussion on this topic will follow in the reflections for this section.

The Forbidding of Oaths

Another distinctive of the Anabaptists is their forbidding of swearing oaths. Put simply,

> no oaths are to be sworn, in accordance with the teaching of Christ and of James. For all words and actions should be confirmed by a solemn Yes or No, without anything further, and this speaking with the truth is to be esteemed as a sworn oath (CC).

While they acknowledged that the Old Testament accepted oaths, "there entered in diverse abuses (through human hypocrisy)." As a result, Jesus "has entirely abolished and forbidden all aforementioned swearing of oaths (whether they were done freely or hypocritically)." "In its place he has commanded all his listeners and disciples to only say 'yes' and 'no' (according to the truth)" (33A). Menno Simons, in *Confession of the Distressed Christians*, elaborates on this change by referring to the time of the Law, which allowed oaths as "the dispensation of imperfectness."

Suffering

Like the early church, the Anabaptists experienced suffering and martyrdom. Also like the early church, they developed a strong theology of suffering. Klaassen highlights two distinct forms of suffering which the Anabaptists described: "the internal suffering which is caused by the slow liberation from dependence on created things and the external suffering of persecution." Both "are understood as part of the cross of Christ, not something done for Christ, but something done with Christ. The disciple shares in the cross as a co-sacrifice" (AIO 4.0).

While the idea of carrying one's cross and dying to one's sins is a universal one in Christian teaching, not every church tradition in every place has developed a strong theology of suffering as the result of persecution—largely because not every church tradition was developed in the midst of suffering at the hands of external forces.

Thus, Anabaptist confessions which claim that Christ's people "have crucified their flesh with all its lusts and desires" (SA) and that God has given us power to "crucify the old being in us, becoming like him in his suffering and death" (SC) would not seem too out of step with Western Protestants.

However, the statement that Christ gave his life for us "that we might also be willing to give our body and life for Christ's sake, which means for the sake of all the brothers" (CO) might seem somewhat strange to contemporary Western Christians.

But the claim that "those born of Christ... follow him to the cross where there is oppression, scorn and suffering" (KC) is very much outside of the experience of Christians in America today. Even in Europe and Canada, where secularism and censorship of traditional religious ideas is on the rise, the experience of Christians there cannot meaningfully compare to that of the early Anabaptists.

It was in this context of suffering and martyrdom—banishment, burning, beheading, drowning, and torture unimaginable by all modern people apart from the sociopathic—that the Anabaptists told their people to expect "to suffer oppression and scorn from all people" (KC).

Jakob Hutter, the founder of the Hutterites who was tortured and then burned at the stake, wrote to those under his influence to

> not be ashamed of the bonds and suffering of Christ, but rejoice greatly in your hearts, for you know that nothing else has been promised you for your life on earth except suffering and death, tribulation, anxiety, distress and great persecution, pain, torture, insult and shame at the hands of godless men. That is the true sign and seal of all the pious children of God, the sign of Christ or the Son of Man and all his members which must appear at the last time according to the word of the Lord. Yes, cross and tribulation truly adorns all the children of God (AIO 4.10).

By stating that only Christians who suffer are the true children of God, Hutter was implying that the Christians who made them suffer were not children at all. Christ, the head, suffered and died, thus why should we assume that "the members of Christ would not need to suffer just like the head" (LMS 7)? "Let this mind be in you," Simons similarly exhorted, "which was also in Christ Jesus. Now Christ Jesus was minded to suffer; and in the same way all Christians must be minded" (BJL).

The Proclamation of the Gospel (Missiology)

The early Anabaptist confessions speak occasionally of evangelism. The Kempen Confession, for instance, states that "we wish nothing but to seek alone the salvation of our souls and, like Christ, seek the well-being of the souls and lives of all people" (KC). The Waterlander Confession also speaks of evangelism in the context of church discipline—arguing that an unrepentant brother "shall be separated and cut off from the body of Christ to God's honor; that his church may remain pure and an instrument for the conversion of the fallen" (WC).

However, the concept of missionary work is not given significant attention in these early confessions. Fast forward to today and many evangelicals who argue for the importance of missions will use conservative Anabaptist groups like the Amish as a negative example, e.g. "we can't be like the Amish who separate themselves from society; we have to go out there and win souls for Jesus!"

One might assume from these data points that early Anabaptists did not expend much effort thinking about and engaging in missions work. However, this is not the case.

As early as 1527, the Missionary Conference of Augsburg sent out Anabaptist brothers to different cities in Switzerland, Austria, and Germany to proclaim the gospel. Almost all of these missionaries were killed shortly after arriving, thus providing the other name this conference is known by—the Martyrs' Synod.

This work continued in various Anabaptist communities. Anabaptist missionaries were often sent out in teams to preach and read the Bible to groups in homes and barns. Some Anabaptist churches even had commissioning services where those who believed they had a calling to share the gospel would be formally offered support by the congregation and sent out. Pledges were made by fellow congregants to care for widows and orphaned children in the not-unlikely event that a missionary would be martyred for the cause. A hymn written for one of these commissioning services included this stanza:

> As God his Son was sending
> Into this world of sin,
> His Son is now commanding
> That we this world should win.
> He sends us and commissions
> To preach the gospel clear,
> To call upon all nations
> To listen and to hear.[3]

Whether in their own country or in another, Anabaptists were known to engage in public proclamations, secret meetings, and illegal baptisms. Formal Anabaptist missions predates Protestant efforts, though early Anabaptist efforts were largely focused on bringing Catholics and Protestants into conformity with what they understood to be the New Testament faith as opposed to reaching the unchurched.

In contrast to the missionary efforts of Catholics and Protestants in the first few hundred years after the Reformation, which were tainted by colonialism and military conquest, Anabaptist evangelism and missionary work was done without violence. Thus Hubmaier's statement that

> the slayers of heretics are the worst heretics of all, in that they, contrary to Christ's teaching and practice, condemn heretics to the fire. By pulling up the harvest prematurely they destroy the wheat along with the tares... A Turk or a heretic cannot be persuaded by us either with the sword or with fire, but only with patience and prayer (AIO 15.1).

3. Shenk, *Anabaptism and Mission*, 63

Reflections

Community

Each modern Anabaptist group tends to have confidence that their model of community is best, but the variety of applications of the Anabaptist values of community, separation, shunning, and simplicity suggests that there may not be one perfect approach and that each model has its benefits and drawbacks.

For instance, while the Amish benefit from their skepticism toward popular culture by not falling prey to the consumerism and hedonism of the contemporary West, they must sacrifice individual conscience to group conscience regarding what kind of technologies are acceptable and beneficial—even if the group could be mistaken.

And while the Hutterite emphasis on sharing and simplicity creates a sense of belonging and purpose, its clearly defined roles and limited work opportunities can also be very restrictive to those with godly ambitions that don't fit neatly into their community's goals and values.

These movements have at times been romanticized as the solution to all of the problems which face the modern West, but the truth is more complicated. Some of these separatist communities are also prone to authoritarian leadership, pride, and legalism. In more regulated fellowships, communal discipline can become a means for the powerful to dominate others for personal or political reasons, not the expression of love that early Anabaptists intended for it to be.

Another problem that increasingly faces Anabaptist communities after the first generation is false profession of faith. In its early years, to be an Anabaptist was to choose to convert. One was drawn in from the outside, generally by a strong desire to follow Christ no matter the cost. As time went on, however, children were born into the movement without really choosing it for themselves. The merely carnal influences of familial and social pressures motivate them to fall in line. They also fear leaving the fellowship to go to an outside world they don't understand and don't know how to succeed in. Thus, they stay for reasons other than the attractiveness of Christ and their desire to follow him. For these cultural Anabaptists, the supposedly difficult life of separation and sacrifice becomes a broad way that they can travel more easily than the "narrow way" of having to navigate the strange worldliness outside of the community. This kind of unconverted Anabaptism, where external adherence to cultural norms overshadows internal love for God and neighbor, can also make life together less than the ideal we hope it will be. Wheat and chaff grow up together and shape the community and its culture. Even Anabaptist communities become divided into the visible and invisible church.

None of these problems necessarily makes choosing life in close, separated community the wrong choice. However, one must be realistic about trade-offs and understand that there is no perfect community because there are no perfect people. Hutterite and Amish life are one possible expression of Anabaptist values like unity, simplicity, and separation, but they are not the only expressions of it. Nevertheless, their examples can inspire us to commit ourselves to the body of Christ and to separate from corrupting influences of the world.

Simplicity

The difficulty with applying the tenet of simplicity is that it means different things in different contexts. In a wealthy country, simplicity might mean reducing clutter and rejecting crass consumerism. But for Anabaptists living in poorer economic conditions, material considerations are largely about having enough to survive and a little extra to share with the brothers and sisters. There is no one standard for what simplicity looks like, so individuals and communities must navigate what it means to live simply within their own contexts. Nevertheless, this work should be done because it causes us to reflect upon what it means to live for Christ as opposed to living for things.

Separation

A modern Anabaptist might experience some turmoil over the question of whether their forebears' insistence upon separation went too far in seeing Protestants and Catholics as not just off-base, but teaching damnable heresy. The fact that Anabaptists are not generally martyred by other professing Christians today makes it easier to maintain a friendly, ecumenical attitude toward non-Anabaptist Christians and to extend a hand of fellowship. But when the movement began, Protestants and Catholics not only engaged in violence, but they turned their swords against sincere Anabaptist Christians.

On the other hand, Anabaptism did not emerge in a vacuum. Its members relied on the insights of the Catholic and Protestant churches in many ways. Is it possible that these other Christians were actually fellow, sincere Christians despite being mistaken on significant issues?

The Anabaptist doctrine of separation poses other challenges as well—such as whether an Anabaptist today can be integrated into mainstream society or if we should instead be cloistering ourselves in communities which are literally or metaphorically walled off from the world around us. We cannot fall prey to worldly influences, but isn't there also a danger that separation might lead to pride and hinder evangelism? While separation may be an Anabaptist distinctive, it might be better to think of it as the natural result of holy living and not something to be pursued in its own right.

Holiness

From a biblical perspective, holiness means separation. God and his people are holy because they are distinct from the world and what is common. But this holiness is not separation for its own sake. Holiness also means taking on the character of Jesus. Holiness is life-giving and good.

Christians are holy because God's holiness flows through us from our union with Christ and the Holy Spirit living inside of us. This reality changes our attitudes and behavior when we cooperate.

However, there is a danger of losing our focus on union with God by turning holiness into a mere list of dos and don'ts which we try to obey by our own power. Modern Anabaptists should therefore recall what the earliest brothers and sisters taught about union with Christ and works of love.

We can also learn from traditions outside of Anabaptism. Eastern Orthodox Christians, for instance, developed the doctrine of theosis or "divinization" to describe the sanctification of believers. This doctrine teaches that while Christians remain creations, we participate in God's divine energies, thus becoming in a sense like God by grace. Methodists use the language of sanctification and holiness to describe their distinct emphasis on living a changed life. Impressed by this teaching, the Brethren in Christ denomination added to their Anabaptism a conscious effort to include Methodist teaching about Spirit-enabled sanctification to complement and enforce the Anabaptist emphasis on holy living. Modern Anabaptists should be open to life-changing truths no matter where they originate.

Suffering

The Kempen Confession says that those born of Christ "follow him to the cross where there is oppression, scorn and suffering, as Christ himself speaks and testifies" (KC). This raises an important question: are true believers *always* persecuted by the world? If so, can one be a Christian in a free society?

The Gospels predict oppression for Christians, and they surely had their share of it in their first three hundred years. The early Anabaptists likewise suffered, though with pockets of toleration in various times and places. This led them to suggest that suffering is guaranteed to those who truly follow Jesus.

But were they right? Is suffering guaranteed, or is it just one way that Satan seeks to tear down Christ's church? Could prosperity be another diabolical temptation to abandon following Christ?

One of the dangers of teaching Christians to expect suffering is that when we don't experience it, we will be tempted to invent it in order to maintain our sense of self as *real* followers of Christ. While we can expect to suffer internally for following Jesus when following is difficult, whether or not others will try to oppress us is not so much dependent upon us but upon them. External oppression will come and go, but all Christians must take up their cross and follow Jesus along the often difficult but rewarding path of obedience.

This is the kind of suffering which we should say is guaranteed to our brothers and sisters, and we should seek to encourage them through it. And if oppression should come, the love of the Christian community can give us strength.

Shunning

When compared to the violence which Protestants and Catholics inflicted against dissidents, the nonviolent church discipline such as shunning which the Anabaptists used would have been seen as a rather progressive and perhaps even soft approach to keeping Christians in line. However, shunning is not seen that way today. In the contemporary West, where voluntary religion is now treated as a given, shunning is seen not as progressive or compassionate but as harsh and manipulative. Moreover, shunning is presented as counterproductive because it can unintentionally push members into the arms of alternative communities which are not necessarily concerned with Christian spiritual formation.

While this can be true of shunning today, it was not true in the 16th century. A believing Anabaptist had already excluded himself from mainstream society, thus he or she relied on the brotherhood to survive. The threat of being cut off from that support system created significant pressures to fall back in line. Likewise, in the early church, which operated in a collectivist context in which each person relied on a network of support, being shunned by the community of faith could also bring a Christian into line quite effectively. In our modern context, when a shunned person can always go to the church next door, some might ask whether such an approach remains effective.

If the motivation of church discipline is truly to love a wayward brother or sister, as the early Anabaptist confessions proclaim, then it should only be implemented when it can be used as a loving means toward a loving end. Otherwise, it will be perceived as harsh judgmentalism that pushes believers out into the world to be cut off from Christ.

Gender Hierarchy

While it's not surprising that early Anabaptists had a tendency to follow their culture in imposing a gender hierarchy within marriage that was not necessarily rooted in biblical concerns, this is an area which modern Anabaptists should revisit using the insights of modern, faithful biblical scholarship and a desire to follow the early church's radical egalitarian philosophy—a philosophy which earned them opprobrium from their contemporaries and caused them to be dismissed as following a religion for women and slaves.

Sincere, biblically oriented Christians continue to debate the importance of gender roles within marriage and in the church—for instance, the Brethren in Christ denomination has welcomed female pastors into ministry for decades without compromising their belief in biblical inspiration. However, Riedemann's comparison of wives to the flesh which must be controlled and mastered betrays a particularly unhelpful anthropology. Nevertheless, the early Anabaptist belief in the freedom of women to marry or stay single is a brighter spot in their theology of gender.

Satan and the State

Another significant area for growth in Anabaptist thought has to do with the Anabaptist understanding of human governments.

While acknowledging a sinful human element in government, a large amount of emphasis in early Anabaptist thought is placed on Rom 13's assertion that the magistrate is an unknowing servant of God. This claim needs to be revisited and perhaps qualified in these ways:

1. In Rom 13, Paul argues, "Let everyone be subject to the governing authorities, for there is no authority except that which God has established. The authorities that exist have been established by God... For rulers hold no terror for those who do right, but for those who do wrong." However, Paul knew full well from both personal and national experience that rulers *are* in fact a terror to those who do good. This brings us to two distinct but not necessarily contradictory conclusions: that Paul is speaking of what rulers are supposed to do but often don't, and/or that Paul may be using irony to subtly critique rulers in a way that his oppressed audience would understand.[4]

2. Early Anabaptists, and modern Anabaptists who seek to imitate their forebears, often leave out a third element in the political process which is strongly testified to in the Bible[5]— the Satanic/demonic element. One notable exception to this trend can be found in Michael Sattler, who wrote, "[Christ] has no kingdom in the world, but that which is of this world is against His kingdom... The devil is prince over the whole world, in whom all the children of darkness rule" (LMS 1). Greater acknowledgment of the infernal influence upon politics would better reflect both the biblical doctrine and the practical realities of sin and oppression which the early Anabaptists suffered under on behalf of the rulers of their day.

4. This second possibility is argued for in detail in Carter, "Irony."

5. See Deut 32:8–9 in the DSS and LXX or as translated in the ESV, Ps 82, Dan 10, Rev 13, etc. Further elaboration on this point is given in Cook, *Fight the Powers.*

4. Last Things (Eschatology)

MOST OF THE EARLY Anabaptists believed they were in the end times. It's not difficult to see why—they were being martyred with some regularity by a political-religious system which had seemingly abandoned the teachings of Jesus, echoing the book of Revelation.

However, this confidence that they were in the last days led to the creation of false prophecies which misled many in the movement. The most extreme example of this took place when Matthijs and van Leiden led a violent rebellion in Münster in order to make it into the New Jerusalem, believing that the time for peace was over now that the end was near. This effort predictably ended in tragedy and slaughter. It also led later Anabaptists like Marpeck and Simons to avoid prediction making, although even prior to the Münster debacle the Martyr's Synod had already asked Hans Hut to stop setting dates for the end of the world.

Hubmaier likewise maintained that "the day of the Lord is nearer to us than we expect," however,

> concerning this I very strongly opposed Hans Hut and his followers when they hoodwinked the simple people by claiming a definite time for the last day, namely next Pentecost. They convinced them to sell their property and leave wife and child, house and field behind, and are now without means of support. Thus the poor people were convinced to follow him by a seductive error which arose out of ignorance of Scripture (AIO 17.9).

Perhaps partly due to the false predictions of Hut and the tragedy at Münster, the early confessions represent a more general eschatology which broadly follows the contours of the New Testament. Thus, we read about "the bodily resurrection of the dead, both of the just and the unjust" (CC), where each person's "body shall be united with the departed soul" (WC) on the day of judgment when "everyone will be judged in accordance with their deeds" (CC) and go their separate ways: "the good to eternal life, the evil to eternal punishment" (WC). "Those who have not died but remain alive upon earth shall be changed in a moment into an eternal state" (SC) "after the likeness of Christ" (33A).

This day will not be expected, but will overtake us like "a thief in the night" (33A). The Thirty-Three Articles engages in a bit of speculation, picturing that "the earth, waters and brooks shall be changed into burning pitch and sulphur, which shall burn from eternity to eternity" (33A). It is unclear from this depiction if the earth will ever be restored and have the New Jerusalem come down to it, as depicted in Revelation or if they believed the damned would stay on earth while the redeemed would live in heaven. Since the confession goes on to say that damned "shall be left here and be cast into the aforementioned pool of darkness," the latter seems likely.

Anabaptists also awaited the destruction of the corrupt earthly kingdoms that oppressed the people of God: "God will destroy all the earthly, the visible regime and burn it with an eternal fire; but will exclude humans who have carried out the will of God and who will thus live into eternity" (33A).

Simons similarly wrote that

> all those who pursue us [shall] be as ashes under the soles of our feet and they shall acknowledge too late that emperor, king, duke, prince, crown, scepter, majesty, power, sword, and mandate, were nothing but earth, dust, wind, and smoke. With this day in view, all afflicted and oppressed Christians who now labor under the cross of Christ are comforted in the firm hope of the life to come; and they leave all tyrants with their heathenish mandates to God and his judgment (AIO 17.28).

The Münster rebels, along with the Protestant and Catholic leaders, believed that it was their duty to kill heretics, but Simons countered them with Jesus' parable of the wheat and the tares (Matt 13):

> The good seed are the children of the kingdom; but the tares are the children of the wicked one; the enemy that sowed them is the devil, the harvest is the end of the world; and the reapers are the angels. Inasmuch as the Christians are the good seed, how then can they be the angels or reapers? Or if they be the reapers, how can they be the seed? These two things, the seed and the reapers, are quite different. Its plainness must not be obscured...

> These angels will be the reapers who at the end of the world, that is in the day of judgment, will root up all tares and cast them into the lake of fire. Until that time the tares will be left among the good seed and the goats with the sheep. Let none think that we should now root up the tares, or that we should now separate the goats from the sheep. For when the Son of Man shall come in his glory and all his holy angels with him, then shall he sit upon the throne of his glory: and before him shall be gathered all nations: and he shall separate them one from another, as a shepherd divideth his sheep from the goats: and he shall set the sheep on his right hand, but the goats on the left (BJL).

Thus, judgment is in the hands of God, not men. Christians may often be martyrs, but they should never be oppressors.

Finally, another emphasis that can be found in Anabaptist eschatology is a "now, but not yet" eschatology. We see this in particular in their ethics, which call Christians to act as if Christ and his kingdom have already completely overcome the world, even though we still await its full consummation. Unlike their Catholic and Protestant counterparts, Anabaptists believed that Isaiah's prophecy had in one sense already come to pass, thus Christians "have changed their carnal weapons, their swords, into ploughshares and their spears into sickles. They neither lift a sword, nor teach, nor participate in carnal warfare" (SC).

Conclusion

IN THE FINAL ANALYSIS, Anabaptist theology is perhaps about love. It begins with the love of God for all of humanity which led the Father to send the Son to bring us back into communion with him.

God's love for us inspires us to love him. This love demonstrates itself in our obedience. We also love the brethren by participating in fellowship with them, sharing our earthly goods with them, and helping them to better follow Jesus.

Finally, the love of God refracts through us and shines onto the world, to whom we preach the gospel and refuse to retaliate against when they persecute us because of Christ.

In all of these things, love does not coerce. God does not force us to believe and follow; we are given a choice. Christian brothers do not use the threat of violence to keep each other in line, but the means of persuasion. Finally, Christian evangelism is an offer to be received voluntarily or not at all by those who are willing to commit themselves to following Christ.

While the ethical and practical dimensions of the Anabaptist faith are perhaps more central than in other Christian traditions, it is by no means the case that the early Anabaptists had no concern for the proper expression of their theology in words. For them to be willing to die for the faith, they had to understand the content of that faith, which meant it must be formulated and expressed. Their confessions, rooted in Scripture and inspired by the Apostles' Creed, helped them to do just this.

Bibliography

Bender, Harold S. *The Anabaptist Vision*. Scottdale, PA: Herald, 1944. Kindle edition.

Carter, T. L. "The Irony of Romans 13." *Novum Testamentum* 46.3 (2004) 209–28. https://doi.org/10.1163/1568536041528213.

Cook, Cody. *Fight the Powers*. Cincinnati: Cantus Firmus Media, 2018.

Fudge, Edward. *The Fire That Consumes: A Biblical and Historical Study of the Doctrine of Final Punishment*. 3rd ed. Eugene, OR: Cascade, 2011.

Giles, Kevin. *The Eternal Generation of the Son: Maintaining Orthodoxy in Trinitarian Theology*. Downers Grove, IL: IVP Academic, 2012. Kindle edition.

Gupta, Nijay K., and John K. Goodrich, eds. *Sin and Its Remedy in Paul*. Eugene, OR: Cascade, 2020. Kindle edition.

Klaassen, Walter, ed. *Anabaptism in Outline*. Walden, NY: Plough, 2019.

Koop, Karl, ed. *Confessions of Faith in the Anabaptist Tradition: 1527–1676*. Walden, NY: Plough, 2019. Kindle edition.

Marpeck, Pilgram. *The Writings of Pilgram Marpeck*. Translated by William Klassen and Walter Klaassen. Walden, NY: Plough, 2019.

McGrath, William R. "The Anabaptists: Neither Catholic nor Protestant." 1956. https://anabaptistfaith.org/anabaptists-neither-catholic-nor-protestant/.

Menno Simons. *The Complete Writings of Menno Simons: C. 1496–1561*. Edited by J. C. Wenger. Translated by Leonard Verduin. Scottdale, PA: Herald, 1984.

Nazianzen, Gregory. "Letters (Division I)." https://www.newadvent.org/fathers/3103.htm.

Riedemann, Peter. *Love Is Like Fire: The Confession of an Anabaptist Prisoner*. Edited by Emmy Barth Maendel. Walden, NY: Plough, 2016.

———. *Peter Riedemann's Hutterite Confession of Faith*. Translated by John Friesen. Walden, NY: Plough, 2019.

Sattler, Michael. *The Legacy of Michael Sattler*. Edited by John Howard Yoder. Walden, NY: Plough, 2019.

Shenk, Wilbert R. *Anabaptism and Mission*. Scottdale, PA: Herald, 1984.

Wolfe, Stephen. *The Case for Christian Nationalism*. Moscow, ID: Canon, 2022.